DISCARDED

HUMBOLDT STATE

Date Due

D1108066

MEDIEVAL HUMANISM

THE CHRISTENDOM SERIES

OTHER VOLUMES IN THIS SERIES WILL
BE ANNOUNCED LATER

MEDIEVAL HUMANISM

By Gerald Groveland Walsh, S.J.

PROFESSOR OF MEDIEVAL CULTURE
FORDHAM UNIVERSITY
EDITOR OF "THOUGHT"

New York · 1942
THE MACMILLAN COMPANY

Imprimi potest
James P. Sweeney, S.J.
Provincial, Md.-N.Y.

December 14, 1940.

Nihil obstat
Arthur J. Scanlan, S.T.D.
Censor Librorum.

Imprimatur
✠ Francis J. Spellman, D.D.
Archbishop, New York.

December 22, 1940.

Copyright, 1942, by
THE MACMILLAN COMPANY.

All rights reserved—no part of this book
may be reproduced in any form without
permission in writing from the publisher,
except by a reviewer who wishes to quote brief
passages in connection with a review written
for inclusion in magazine or newspaper.

First Printing.

B
738
H8
W3

PRINTED IN THE UNITED STATES OF AMERICA

THE CHRISTENDOM SERIES

Editors

CARLTON J. H. HAYES
HERBERT C. F. BELL
EUGENE H. BYRNE
MARSHALL W. BALDWIN
WILLIAM M. AGAR
REV. T. LAWRASON RIGGS
ROSS J. S. HOFFMAN, *Chairman*

PREFACE

THIS little book contains the substance of a series of lectures on the Tradition of Christian Humanism, which were given in 1939–40, as a Fordham University extension course, at the College of New Rochelle. Many paragraphs are direct transcripts from the notes which Mother Grace, O.S.U., of that College, has kindly put at my disposal.

I am indebted to my friend Ross Hoffman, of the Fordham University Graduate School, for the enthusiastic encouragement without which the book would never have been put together; and to Professor Marshall W. Baldwin, of New York University, for his painstaking reading of the manuscript and for some valuable suggestions and important corrections. For permission to quote from Don Sturzo's *Church and State* I am indebted to Longmans, Green & Company; and to Richard R. Smith, Inc., for permission to quote Robin Flower's "Pangur Bán."

It must be remembered that in so slight an essay the humanistic tradition has had to be looked at in isolation from the total pattern of medieval culture and religion. The author is, of course, well aware of the evidence of other elements in the rich reality of medieval life. His justification is that the particular tradition here studied has been unwarrantably neglected in most of the manuals of medieval history.

G.G.W.

CONTENTS

MEDIEVAL HUMANISM

CHAPTER I

THE TRADITION OF CHRISTIAN HUMANISM

HUMANISM, in general, I take to be the idea that a human being is meant to achieve, during life, a fair measure of human happiness.[1] It implies, of course, that happiness is to be sought in a human way. It supposes, that is, that a man should seek happiness without being lifted to the level of the angels or lowered to that of the brutes. It proposes a way that reconciles with one another the demands of intelligence, conscience and taste. Intelligence seeks for happiness through truth; conscience, for happiness through what is right, just, good; taste, for happiness through what is beautiful. It is possible, also, to seek for happiness through physical pleasure; and undoubtedly a good deal of happiness can be found that way. But one need not be a solemn moralist to observe that human experience, from the time of Solomon (to go no further back), has made it sufficiently clear that happiness sought in pleasure alone does not long satisfy human nature. Happiness has been sought, with some success, in truth

[1] See *Adversity's Noblemen* (The Italian Humanists on Happiness), by C. E. Trinkaus, Columbia University Press, 1940.

alone or in justice alone or in beauty alone, as plenty of philosophers, reformers and artists have lived to attest. But there would seem to be a risk in deliberately limiting the music of life to a single string, however lovely the note may be. Everyone knows the tragic page in Darwin's Diary where he records that he sacrificed one by one all his young ardors for music and poetry and drama to his single love of (what he hoped would be) scientific truth. With the possible exception of Saints and creative geniuses, it seems fairly established that men who are eager for human happiness must seek it in several ways.

What Christian humanism adds to pagan humanism is the idea that the several ways of seeking human happiness will best be reconciled when one ekes out reason with Revelation in the search for truth, conscience with Divine counsels and commandments in the search for righteousness, taste with supernatural Grace in the search for beauty. More briefly, Christian humanism supplements pagan humanism by the ideas of Creation, Incarnation, Sanctification. If the things we can see and the thoughts we can think are true or good or beautiful, then it should be obvious that the Creator of these things must be even more worth the search than the things He created. Hence, Christian humanism seeks for happiness not merely by ordering the senses for the sake of the soul, but also by ordering the soul for the glory of God.

Taken in a large and accommodated sense, a text in the Gospel of St. Luke might serve as a convenient formula of Christian humanism. Jesus Christ, the

Incarnate Word, "grew in wisdom and age and grace with God and man." [2] Whatever be the literal meaning of *sophia,* according to a rigorous exegesis of the Greek text, "wisdom" may be taken to suggest that which when loved makes us "philosophers," lovers of wisdom, pursuers of happiness through truth. It was this pursuit that gives a special character to Hellenic culture, to the culture that reached its fullness in a man like Plato. "Age" *(helikia)* may be taken to mean that kind of wisdom that comes by experience, that is learned not by thinking but by living, not by contemplation but by action. It is the kind of wisdom we associate with the Romans, with those practical men who gave to the Western world the most enduring example of life under law, of a social life ordered by accepted and tested norms of right and wrong. Grace *(charis)* is different from human wisdom and human experience chiefly in the sense that it can spring neither from human intelligence nor human conscience, but must come to us as a gift from God. It is like wisdom in so far as it is a light, an illumination, a revelation for the mind. It is like experience, in so far as it is a force, an inspiration, a comforter for the will. Grace is light and love that come directly from God, gratuitously. It adds enormously to the happiness that ordinary truth and justice give.

Our Lord grew in "Grace with God *and men.*" This latter kind of *charis* might perhaps be rendered by our word "charm." Christian charm is the outer manifestation of that inward balance, poise, harmony that results from the cultivation of intelligence, conscience and taste

[2] Luke, ii, 52.

in the light of both reason and Revelation and in the force of both nature and Grace.

Medieval humanism at its best was Christian humanism. There were men in the twelfth and thirteenth centuries who combined a Hellenic passion for the truth with a Roman emphasis on law and a Christian hunger for Divine Life, for communion with God. To all this they added a quality of fancy and feeling, more rarely found in the life and literature of Greece and Rome but common enough among peoples of Celtic or Teutonic strains. Thus we shall find an Abelard (1079–1142), with an intelligence as luminous as a Greek's, writing moral advice as solemnly as Seneca after loving Heloise as passionately as Tristram had loved Isolde; and then turning to hymn writing in the mood of a Teuton, the music of a Celt and the manner of a Saint. In St. Thomas Aquinas (1225–1274), everyone now recognizes one of the world's supreme intelligences. But his conscience was as delicate as his intelligence was acute; and he was no less a lover of beauty than he was a lover of truth and goodness. He was a philosopher, a Saint and an artist all in one. Or take Dante (1265–1321). One thinks of him, primarily, as a supreme artist; but he was so much more than this. "Even the most passionate and original characters of modern times," writes Karl Vossler, "appear, in comparison with the mediaeval Titan, somehow artificial." [3] The two men, taken together, represent an enormous range of human living; and certainly justify the attempt to trace, however briefly, the tradition of Christian humanism, from

[3] *Mediaeval Culture,* vol. I, p. 349 (New York, 1929).

its beginnings to its climax in the thirteenth century.

It is said in the Gospel that Our Lord *grew* in wisdom and age and grace. *Proficiebat.* He made progress, as we would say. And that is true of Christian humanism in general. It was not achieved in a day or a single generation. Nor is it something that ever becomes settled, solidified, susceptible of an irreformable definition. It is a historical, not a logical, reality; it presents itself in each generation as a process, not as a final and perfect product. However much the substance or essence remains the same, the shape and accidentals vary with time and place. Even within Christendom it has had to battle for its right to exist; it has been mistrusted, mistreated, misunderstood. Not all Christians have realized the magnitude of Christ's gift of humanism, nor has the non-Christian world been ready to yield up its cultural treasures to the Church without a struggle.

The problem of Christian humanism produced a crisis in the conscience of many converts in the first two centuries of our era. Why bother, they asked, with wisdom, with *sophia,* when one has Grace, *charis*? This fear of Athens, of philosophy, of intelligence pursuing happiness in truth, haunted and has continued to haunt many a Christian soul—as though rational truth were a distraction drawing men away from their supernatural destiny!

A second crisis occurred when the leaders in the Church sought to incorporate the sounder elements of Roman civilization as they had already absorbed the substance of Greek culture. When the double struggle was over, when Greek logic and Roman law were inseparable from Christian life, when culture and civilization and religion were parts of a single whole, the world of the fourth century witnessed a synthesis of Catholic sanctity, scholarship and statesmanship that has never been surpassed. It was the age of Basil (330–379) and Gregory Nazianzen (330–390), Ambrose (340–397), Jerome (340–420) and Augustine (354–430), to mention only names of those who have been officially declared Doctors of the Church.

After this splendid efflorescence of Catholic life came a period of transition. We sometimes speak of the period as that of the decline and fall of the Roman Empire. But that is a purely negative view of the age. It was a period that resolutely faced the problem which neither Greek culture nor Roman civilization had ever dared to face: the problem not merely of despising or subduing the Barbarians, but of adopting them as brothers, of welcoming them into the household of Faith, of making them citizens of Christendom, of offering them all they could take from the Church's treasure of *sophia, helikia* and *charis*. A man like Bede (674–735), in eighth-century Northumbria, is the symbol of this marvelous transformation. The Carolingian Renaissance (as it is sometimes called) may have produced men of smaller intellectual and cultural stature than the fourth-century Renaissance; but in many ways it represents the solution of a more difficult problem. It was harder to make men happy in the possession of truth, goodness, beauty and Grace in the eighth and ninth centuries than it was in the fourth and fifth. And, therefore, in the history of Christian humanism, the age of Alcuin (735–804) is highly significant.

There followed the Dark Ages. Not that Christian humanists were altogether lacking or that they were at fault. With ruins all around her, a brave little nun like Hrotswitha (932–1002), in far-off Saxony, lifts up a loud voice in Gandersheim (*clamor validus Gandersheimensis* she calls herself), and tells the world that visions may be seen and verses may be written even though most of the teachers are dead.

In the eleventh century, Christian men come out from their cultural catacombs; and in the twelfth, there is another spring, a revirescence of Christian humanism. It is the age of Hildebert of Lavardin (1056–1133), John of Salisbury (1115–1180), Pierre de Blois (1135–1205), and of a dozen others whose astonishing works in prose and verse have been attracting scholars in our generation. This is the century, likewise, of the glorious beginnings of Gothic architecture and of the hardly less glorious achievements of the pioneers in vernacular literature.

With the thirteenth century, we have the mind of St. Thomas (1225–1274) and the music of Dante (1265–1321). But from the point of view of an integral humanism there was a real danger in this and the following centuries. There was in the thirteenth century too exclusive an insistence on logic; as in the fourteenth there was too much preoccupation with law. Professional competence in philosophy and jurisprudence gained enormously, but at the expense of a liberal education. Culture, civilization and religion began to be regarded as products rather than as processes, as professions to be pursued rather than as personal experiences to be lived, as means to fortune rather than as the very sources of happiness.

There was, of course, a reaction to this cold exteriorism. And, as so often in periods of reaction, there was a good deal of extravagance and mere rebelliousness. To recapture the experience of personal religion, men went off into a misdirected or mistaken mysticism. Those who preferred a cozy confidence in the individual and immediate experience of the senses began to mistrust metaphysics. And with nominalism and pseudo-mysticism in the air, the rational synthesis of Scholasticism was replaced by all sorts of sectarian passions.

The humanists of the fifteenth century too often felt that passion for beauty dispensed them from preoccupation with goodness and truth. In the sixteenth century, many who talked of Grace and Glory seemed to forget that there was any other source of human happiness or hope. With the seventeenth century, there was too much of literary classicism and political absolutism, too much of convention and law, and too little of creation and life. In the Enlightenment, intelligence was divorced from conscience and taste, and still more from Grace and Divine Revelation. With the Romantic movement, passion reasserted itself, but at the expense of reason. The Industrial Revolution looked to happiness through physical comfort; and prepared us for the brief but dangerous illusion of atheistic, materialistic Communism.

The world is once more ready for a sane philosophy of human happiness. The story of the struggles to keep humanism alive in the Middle Ages may have for our day a more than purely speculative and archaeological interest.

CHAPTER II

THE ROOTS OF CHRISTENDOM

MEDIEVAL humanism might be described as a synthesis of the fivefold striving after happiness represented by Hellenic intelligence, Roman conscience, Christian Grace, Celtic fancy and Teutonic feeling. The first step in its development was a welding or, better, wedding of Hellenism and Catholicism, of wisdom with Grace, of reason with Revelation, of philosophy with Faith, of human aspiration with supernatural Hope, of natural with Divine love, of *eros* with *charis*, of Plato with Christ.

CATHOLICISM AND HELLENISM

It is on account of this fact that Catholic humanism has ever since been open to a double accusation. On the one hand, it is often said that Catholic humanism is not really Catholic or, at least, not Catholic enough; on the other, it is said that it is not really humanistic, not Greek enough. The first objection cannot be maintained seriously. The Greeks knew nothing about the Mystery of the Incarnation, of the fact that God (without ceasing to be Divine) became man so that man (without ceasing to be human) might become "like" God, might share in a Divine Life, might know and love in a way impossible to man as man. The Greeks, who knew so much about grace, knew nothing about Grace. The Greek soul strove for all sorts of heights and depths of "mystic" intuition, but had no understanding of Faith, of Divine Revelation. It looked wistfully up long avenues of human aspiration, but it had no real hope in Everlasting Life. It explored fully enough the experiences of possessive love, and knew something of pity; but of dedication, of self-surrender, of sacrifice as implied by Christian Charity, the Greek was wholly ignorant. When the Greeks who came to Jerusalem for the Pasch heard Our Lord say: "Amen, amen, I say to you, unless the grain of wheat falling into the ground die, itself remaineth alone, but if it die, it bringeth forth much fruit. He that loveth his life shall lose it, and he that hateth his life in this world keepeth it unto life eternal," [1] their intelligence, so curious and so cultivated, must have been rudely shocked.

The Greek soul, of course, was at last won to Divine Grace, to the sweet reasonableness of Christ, as Our Lord prophesied when He said: "And, I, if I be lifted up from the earth, will draw all things to myself." [2] But the scholarship of nineteenth-century rationalism was never more mistaken than when it identified the Incarnation, Redemption, Resurrection with the rags and tatters of such borrowed mysteries and mythologies as those of Isis, Osiris and Mithra. It is one thing to feel hunger or nostalgia; quite another, to have food or

[1] John, xii, 24.
[2] *Ibid.*, 32.

be at home. The element of Divine Grace makes Christian humanism definitely different from Hellenic culture.

The other objection, that Christian humanism is the denial of Hellenism, has been made with more plausibility. The very words cited above seem evidence enough: "He that hateth his life in this world, keepeth it unto life eternal." With such a principle, it is claimed, Catholicism can never be more than a system of asceticism, an escape from life, a flight from happiness. St. Paul, too, seems to stand for anti-Hellenism, when he wrote for example: "For professing themselves to be wise, they became fools." [3] "Hath not God made foolish the wisdom of this world?" [4]

There is no doubt that texts like these have been cited even by Catholics, as though such texts implied a positive contempt for the human pursuit of truth and goodness and beauty. The result has been that professional non-Catholic scholars can make declarations like this: "Christianity, as an institutionalized religion, has laid no stress upon the pursuit of truth. Indeed for the most part it has been suspicious of truth seeking processes. . . . It has also, in the main, been the foe of beauty-for-its-own-sake." [5]

The best reply to both Catholics and non-Catholics who have misunderstood Catholic humanism is the massive reply of the historical fact of the tradition that goes from Justin Martyr (105–166) and Minucius Felix

[3] Romans, i, 22.
[4] I Cor., i, 20.
[5] Overstreet, H. A., *The Enduring Quest* (N. Y., 1931), p. 162.

(fl.175) to Basil (330–379) and Augustine (354–430), from Boethius (c.475–525) and Cassiodorus (c.480–c.575) to Bede (674–735) and Alcuin (c.735–804), from Anselm (1033–1109) and Hildebert (c.1056–1133) to St. Thomas (1225–1274) and Dante (1265–1321); and, in the modern world, from St. Thomas More (1478–1535), through John Henry Newman (1801–1890), to all who make profession of Catholic humanism today.

St. Paul, himself, can in fact be claimed as a Christian humanist. In giving the Cross to the Greeks he had no intention of taking away their culture. When he made his first speech in Athens, he spoke not merely as an evangelist but as a philosopher and litterateur; he appealed to pure reason; he cited their poet Aratus: ". . . as some also of your own poets said: For we are also his offspring." [6] When St. Paul converted the Athenians to the Faith, he offered them not less wisdom but more wisdom. It was not because the Greeks loved truth, but because some of them had "changed the truth of God into a lie," [7] that St. Paul reproached them. He had nothing but praise for the Greek philosophy that could argue from nature to God, from "the things that are made" to God's "eternal power and divinity." It was only because, "When they knew God, they have not glorified Him as God or given thanks, but became vain in their thoughts, and their foolish heart was darkened . . . and because they liked not to have God in their knowledge," that he used harsh

[6] Acts, xvii, 28.
[7] Romans, i, 25.

words. It was not Hellenism that St. Paul disliked, but only such Greeks as,

> were filled with all iniquity, malice, fornication, av-
> arice, wickedness, full of envy, murder, contention,
> deceit, malignity, whisperers, detractors, hateful to
> God, contumelious, proud, haughty, inventors of evil
> things, disobedient to parents, foolish, dissolute, with-
> out mercy; who, having known the justice of God, did
> not understand that they who do such things are
> worthy of death.[8]

Christian humanism, in a word, in giving us Heaven does not take away the earth. *Non eripit mortalia qui regna dat celestia.* This was the spirit that directed the efforts of those who first proved that Hellenism had nothing to lose and everything to gain by being "brought into the Temple." [9]

When, with St. Augustine, the synthesis was com-plete, we arrive at a description of the integral human-ist, of the man who is wholly at peace with himself, combining temporal happiness with eternal hope.

> Those who are at peace with themselves *(pacifici in
> semetipsis)*, with their passions in order, subject to
> reason, mind, spirit, and their carnal concupiscences
> put into harness, make up the Kingdom of God. This
> Reign of God means that all things are in order, that
> what in man is highest (and in the best sense human)
> is given control, and whatever we have in common
> with beasts is made to obey; while, at the same time,
> man's most human excellence, his mind and reason,
> is subject to a more powerful sway, to the very Truth

[8] *Ibid.*, i, 29–32.
[9] Acts, xxi, 28.

incarnate, to the Only-begotten Son of God. For man will not control what is below him unless he obey what is above him. And this is the peace which is possible on earth for men of good will; this is the life of the man of supreme and perfect wisdom.[10]

As medieval humanism took root, this ideal of temporal and eternal peace, of earthly and Heavenly happiness, was put into a prayer which has ever since been daily on the lips of all who sing or say the Office:

> Lord God, King of Heaven and earth, do Thou deign to direct our ways and to sanctify our souls, to rule and govern, this day, our hearts and bodies, our thoughts and words and deeds according to Thy Law, in carrying out Thy Commandments, so that here and hereafter, with the help of Thy Grace, O Saviour of the world, we may achieve both freedom and salvation.
> (In the Office at Prime)

There are, of course, outside of the New Testament, very few monuments of Christian humanism in the first century of our era. Yet no one can read, to cite but a single example, the first Papal Encyclical, the Letter of Clement to the Church at Corinth,[11] written in the reign of Domitian, about the year 95, without remarking the Pope's obvious enthusiasm for natural nobility and human virtues.

With the second century the record becomes more abundant. A good illustration is the account which St. Justin Martyr (c.105–166) gives us of his conversion to the Church.[12] With one teacher, he strives to make

---

[10] Migne, *Patrologia Latina,* xxxiv, 1245.
[11] Migne, *Patrologia Graeca,* i.
[12] Migne, *Patrologia Graeca,* vi (*Dialogue with Trypho*).

his own the wisdom of Aristotle; with a second, he rises to the level of Plato. But it is only when he finds Faith in Jesus Christ that he feels himself to be fully a philosopher, a lover of perfect wisdom. At each new ascent, the horizon broadened. In no sense did the New Life mean the death of all that was dear before: "Whatever of truth has been uttered by men belongs to us as Christians." And the same might have been said by Justin of goodness and beauty. Later on, Catholic theologians would use the expression, "Grace supposes nature" *(gratia supponit naturam)*. It is in that sense that Catholicism supposes Hellenism.

One of the gems of early Christian literature is a letter [13] written by an otherwise unknown Greek convert to a friend whose name was Diognetos. The whole letter is redolent of a perfect synthesis of culture and *charis;* but one phrase in particular may be quoted: "What the soul is to the body, that are we Christians to the world." Grace is an added principle of life, a further source of happiness. In all human things, says the writer to Diognetos, Christians are like other men. They live in the same parts of the earth, speak the same language, have the same fatherland; they marry and have children; they live under law. What makes them different is something added, not something taken away. They have, for example, more than one country, because everywhere is home to a pilgrim of Eternity. They live "in the flesh but not according to the flesh." Their model is Christ who came to earth not only as "a

[13] Migne, *Patrologia Graeca*, ii, 1172 ff.

man among men," but also as God. In one exclamation, we are given the roots of Christian humanism in the Mystery of the Incarnation: "O immeasurable humanity and charity of God." Humanity and Charity, *philanthropia* and *agape,* love of all that is really human along with love of God—that is Catholic Hellenism.

Not all those early Catholic Hellenists were Greeks. Christian humanism has seldom been better represented than in a Latin writer like Minucius Felix (fl.175), a convert and the author of one of the best apologies of Christian humanism that have ever been written. Even Ernest Renan, suspicious as he was of the ascetic side of Catholicism, had to admit that the *Octavius* of Minucius Felix is a very gem of humanism. In purity of style its Latin is unsurpassed in the second century: a disciplined passion for literary perfection is apparent on every page. And as the dialogue progresses, you feel the charm of ancient manners at their very best: every word and gesture is calm, correct, cultivated, and yet sufficiently lit up with emotion and fancy to remind us that a flame of Christian Faith is burning beneath the surface appearance of classic coldness.

The Christian martyrs, of whom there were many in the second and third centuries, have often enough been represented as men and women of extravagant ideals and unbalanced emotions.[14] It must be confessed that a few of the early biographers and many of the histori-

---

[14] Canon Streeter's reckless charges of "masochism" leveled at a martyr like St. Ignatius of Antioch, in *The Primitive Church,* may serve as an illustration.

ans have written in a way to warrant these charges.
But the more one reads of contemporary accounts, the
more one gains a different impression.

We know, for example, in much detail the end of a
martyr like St. Cyprian (c.200–258). It is impossible
to read the account without thinking of the end of that
other great gentlemen-saint and humanist-martyr,
Thomas More. The inquisition before the Proconsul
Paternus proceeds with as much Roman urbanity as
Christian courage.[15] "Yes, I am a Christian and a
Bishop; I acknowledge no God but the one true God
Who made Heaven and earth. . . . We pray for our-
selves and for all men, for the Emperor too. . . ." In
the subsequent trial before the Proconsul Galerius
Maximus, to the reminder: "The Emperors have ordered you to offer sacrifice," the martyr replies with a
simple, "I cannot obey." The Proconsul begged him to
have a care of himself. "You must carry out orders,"
Cyprian replied, "as for me, my duty is clear, I cannot
deliberate." The judges condemned him to die.
"Thanks be to God," was all the Saint said. Then he
came to the place where he had to die; he took off his
cloak and knelt to pray; next, he took off his coat and
stood with his neck bared waiting for the executioner
to come. When the executioner arrived, Cyprian bade
his friends give the man twenty-five pieces of gold.
Then they brought him the cloth to cover his eyes; he
took it and tied it himself. With the bands for tying his
hands he was content to be helped. "And so," ends the
laconic account, "the blessed Cyprian died." There were

15 Migne, *Patrologia Latina,* iii, 1498 ff.

no scenes, no melodrama, no mere emotionalism; but like a man and a martyr he met his death. It was all, if one may use the word in this connection, in perfect taste. It is impossible not to think of St. Thomas More on the scaffold, joking about his beard, and also of Socrates, playing the game of *kottabos* with the dregs of the goblet of hemlock.

For the best full-length portrait of a Catholic humanist during the period of Christian antiquity, one must turn to the life and writings of St. Basil of Cappadocia (330–379). His tireless search for beauty and truth in all the great centers of culture in his day, his frank association with the pagan professors of Athens who happened to be paragons of scholarship, style and taste, his warm human affection for his friends, his zeal for Christian perfection, his rounded activity as poet, letter-writer, scholar, theologian, pastor of souls and ecclesiastical statesman, his social gifts and personal charm and, of course, his holiness—all these taken together give to his life dimensions, values, integration which neither Hellenic paganism nor modern naturalism could hope to parallel.

Historically, however, it was less the example of Basil than that of the Latin humanists, like St. Ambrose (340–397) and St. Augustine (354–430), that inspired the subsequent development of Catholic culture in the West. St. Augustine's description of the *pacificus,* of the man at peace with himself, of the life of ordered happiness, has already been cited. When he was converted from pride and sensuality (the capital sins, respectively, of Greek culture and Roman civilization) to

Faith and purity, he abdicated none of his rights to specifically human happiness. The Faith showed him new depths of philosophy. Supernatural Hope gave him a new meaning to those inescapable tears and fears that were so puzzling to Manicheism and all forms of pagan pessimism. Divine Charity opened to him new worlds of goodness and beauty. He had found the answer to the cry of his heart, *dilatentur spatia charitatis.* This call for "more love" and Goethe's for "more light" are the two foci about which the ellipse of humanism in every age must turn.

Nothing could be further from the truth than the notion of an Augustine developing into a smug and ascetic Puritan, hostile to that happiness which humanism seeks to achieve through education in the liberal arts. "A young person," he writes, "who neglects the liberal arts may be pious and pure; but so long as he has to live as a man among men, I do not know how anyone can call him happy." [16] It was after, not before, his conversion to Christ that he wrote a little treatise on music,[17] which might be called a very key to humanistic happiness. The theory of poetry which is there sketched is, in reality, a philosophy of human living. In poetry, he says (and it is easy to apply the words to life), there should be music to satisfy the senses, passion to appeal to our emotions, meaning to feed the mind; and all should be lifted to the level of prayer. It was Plato who gave to the world the expression "to live musically," *mousikos zen;* but it was surely Augus-

[16] *De Ordine,* ii, 26 (Migne, *Pat. Lat.,* xxxii, 1011).
[17] Migne, *Pat. Lat.,* xxxii.

tine, the Christian Saint, who has taught us the full meaning of the words.

There has been a good deal of academic debate on the question as to whether men like Augustine and Jerome did not, in reality, renounce their love of literature, as such. The story of St. Jerome being reproached in a dream for being "a Ciceronian" has been repeated endlessly. It is high time this debate should end, once and for all. Anyone who has the illusion that either of these men lost the love for classical literature should read the letters they wrote in their full maturity.[18] They are teeming with classical allusions; and they are written with the most punctilious regard for the literary conventions of rhetoric and rhythmic prose. Those who think that pagan literature is a menace to Christian life write in quite another fashion. The fact is that Plato and Virgil had given to Augustine an ineradicable love for measure and music and all imaginable beauty. He neither could renounce, nor did he feel called upon by his Catholicism to renounce, his passion for the beauty of words. What he feared and detested was falsehood and the "drunken" minds that can pour the wine of error into the loveliest vases of words. It was not because he loved beauty less, but because he loved truth more, that he has sharp words for certain pagan books.

Augustine, like many of his contemporaries, was a complete Catholic humanist. He achieved the fullest possible synthesis between classical culture and the Christian creed and code. He integrated all that is true

[18] For the Letters of Augustine, Migne, *Pat. Lat.*, xxxiii; for those of St. Jerome, *Ibid.*, xxii.

and good and beautiful in the worlds both of nature and Grace. His soul was ever fixed on proportion, harmony, symmetry, unity; because whenever he caught a glimpse of beauty he saw a reflection of the Beauty of God. He knew that it is only when God gives to an artist a share of His own creative power that the world can be enriched by the mystery of an immortal masterpiece in literature, art or life. In this sense Catholic Hellenism is a synthesis of prayer, intelligence and passion, an integral understanding of the three worlds of matter, mind and mystery.

The Faith and the Forum

Catholic intelligence, then, solved the problem of synthesizing a Divine creed with Hellenic culture. A parallel problem was presented to the Catholic conscience: How could Catholic life, with its supernatural code of morals, be reconciled with Roman civilization? How could a Christian civilization be reared on a basis of Roman law, even though a Catholic culture might flourish on the soil of Hellenic logic?

Here, perhaps, is the place to say a word on the meaning of "culture" and "civilization." Culture is a product of social "wisdom," as civilization is a product of social "age" or experience. As historical processes, culture and civilization represent, respectively, the mind and the will, the intelligence and conscience, of society at work. As products, culture is a map for the mind, an order in thoughts, and civilization is a design for living, an order among men and things. Culture springs from the contemplative as civilization from the active life. When groups of men over a number of generations pool their ideas, debate with one another, cancel out errors and reinforce common conclusions, they find that the chemistry of social thinking leaves as a sort of precipitate a pattern of intellectual values. And this pattern in time tends to crystallize as a definite system of thoughts about nature and man and God: the product is some kind of science, philosophy and theology, some sort of theory about the three worlds of matter, and mind, and Mystery. At the same time, such a society will be pooling its experiences and performances; it will be experimenting with means of production and with ways of living together; it will reach some plan for prosperity and some measure of ordered peace. Not, of course, that the pattern of thought or the plan of living is ever a static product. Both culture and civilization are dynamic processes; they are historical realities subject to the law of historical changes. They live and grow and feed on whatever invisible values or material wealth favor organic development.

In the speculative task of ordering invisible thoughts, no city has been so successful as Athens. In the practical business of arranging visible things the genius of Rome was unique. Now, God became man at the very moment when the Roman Plan for Peace had finally incorporated the Hellenic Map for the Mind; so that when Pontius Pilate wrote on the Cross that Jesus Christ was the King of the Jews, he wrote it in Hebrew and Latin and Greek. And indeed, Christ, in His threefold role of Priest, Prophet and Prince, laid equal claim to Jerusalem, Athens and Rome.

The *Pax Romana* was as welcome to St. Peter in Rome as the Greek poetry of Aratus was useful to St. Paul in Athens. Both men were grateful that the Gospel could travel along Roman roads, and that everywhere from Syria to Spain an Apostle of Christ could appeal to a single law and preach in a single tongue. It was as though Divine Providence had arranged the far-flung frontiers of the Roman Empire as a vast cradle for newborn Christendom.

Rome, however, was at first recalcitrant. The persecutions, from Nero (54–68), in the first century, to Diocletian (284–305), in the fourth, attempted to drive Christ from the forum to the catacombs. Under Domitian (81–96), St. John was imprisoned in Patmos; under Trajan (98–117), Ignatius of Antioch (d.107) was to have his flesh ground by the lions, like wheat (as he says) for the making of the Body of Christ; [19] under Marcus Aurelius (161–180), the brave little girl, Blandina (177), the slave,[20] and the philosopher Justin went to their deaths. Decius (249–251), in the third century, reduced persecution to a system; and, to that system, under Valerian (253–260), St. Cyprian, in 258, fell a victim. Finally, Diocletian used every imaginable device to divorce the Faith and Forum. But Christ had conquered; and under Constantine (306–337), the Edict of Toleration (313) announced the victory. By 325, Catholic bishops rode at the Emperor's expense from the far outposts of Britain and Mesopo-

[19] Migne, *Pat. Graeca*, v, 692.
[20] Eusebius, *Ecclesiastical History,* V, 2; *Acta Sanctorum,* June 1, pp. 161 ff.

tamia to proclaim, in the Council of Nicaea, that Christ is truly God and truly man. The efforts of Julian the Apostate (361–364) to strangle the new Catholic civilization with the silken cords of Greek culture had no other effect than to provide for future *Kulturkämpfen* a pattern of persecution that seems perennially destined to failure.

The first fruits of this new Christian civilization were seen in the attitude towards slaves, the sick and the weaker sex. All men and women were now, equally, children of God, persons endowed by the Creator with inalienable rights. And what, perhaps, needs to be noted is that in Christian hospitals the human body, by becoming a Temple of the Holy Ghost, was given not less but more attention than before. Asceticism proved a social asset: private sacrifice meant public service. St. Paul had found the Pagans "without affection, without fidelity, without mercy." [21] "See how they love one another!" [22] was the astonished tribute of the Pagans to the Christians.

The general effects of the fusion of the Faith and the forum have never been more carefully summarized than in a recent work of Don Sturzo, and this must be the excuse for the following lengthy citation:

> The ancient Church did not seek to merge the State into herself nor did she set out to create a civilization of her own by changing the institutions that were her Roman heritage. But in preaching the truths of faith, in the organization of her hierarchy and of worship

[21] Romans, i, 31.
[22] Tertullian, *Apologeticum* (Migne, *Pat. Lat.,* i, 294).

and in the practice of Christian ethics and spirituality, she fulfilled a social function that was in fact a civilizing one. The State remained for her an earthly factor, necessary to the life of the community, yet containing elements contradictory to the spiritual life. Property, wealth, the dominion of certain classes over others, the exercise of force, war, slavery, were likewise to be considered necessary elements of social life, though they sprang from the degeneration of the human race. Such elements, since they could not be suppressed, had to be corrected by the Christian spirit of poverty, humility, abstinence and penance. There remained the innate dualism between the life of the spirit and life of the world in the inner life of the Christian, and between the religious and supernatural ends of the Church and the earthly and social ends of fallen human nature. This dualism, between Church and State in the social sphere, between inner life and political life in the moral sphere, was tending to find a unification in the conception of a natural law.[23]

The Christian Empire was not without its shadows. Some of the bishops, for example, who gained a new role in social and judicial life were tempted by the possession of wealth and power. Felix II (355–65) heads the list of those anti-Popes who were to be elected through political connivance. It became all too easy to enforce the Faith with the aid of political power. The seed of the future Inquisition was sown. The problem of Church and State arose; and continued a matter of debate among Christian men even after St. Thomas Aquinas had settled the matter in the *Summa Theologica*. Dante's *Monarchia* was to be violently attacked,

[23] *Church and State* (N. Y., 1940), p. 44.

as late as the fourteenth century; and it all but led to
the public burning of his bones.

With a man like St. Ambrose of Milan the fusion of
the Faith and the forum reaches a high perfection. Born
in 330 (five years after the Council of Nicaea, in which
Athanasius in the language of Demosthenes and with
the protection of the successor of Caesar Augustus de-
fended the Divinity of Christ), he belonged to the very
highest nobility. He was educated with a view to an
imperial administrative career, and was, in fact, the
Governor of Liguria and Emilia when, by popular de-
mand, he was made the Bishop of Mediolanum (Milan)
in 374. In Ambrose at the age of forty-four there was
the stuff that makes a complete citizen of Christendom:
a careful education in Greek "wisdom," a long experience of Roman ways of acting; aristocratic charm at its
best; and all that held together and lifted to a supernatural level by the Graces of Faith and Hope and Charity.
In the Christian Bishop, all that was best in the Roman
Governor remained. Dedication to God took nothing
away from the energy of the man. His sermons are
careful works of Roman rhetorical art. It was the sheer
literary beauty of his words that first touched the heart
of the young Augustine and won him from heresy and
immorality to humility and purity. *Delectabar suavitate
sermonis,* "I was delighted by the charm of his diction,"
writes Augustine in the *Confessions.*[24] But, of course,
Ambrose was far more than merely charming. His
virile personality dominated three such men as the Emperors Valentinian (364-375), Gratian (375-383),

[24] Book VI.

and Theodosius (379–395). Everyone knows the story,
told by Augustine in the *City of God*,[25] of how the ter-
rible Theodosius, guilty of the savage slaughter of
Thessalonica, was brought to his knees and compelled
by Ambrose to beg for the pardon of God in the pres-
ence of his people. And from that moment on, for the
more than one thousand years of medieval Christendom, political absolutism remained a sin, until with the
revival of paganism in the fifteenth century, the world
began once more to dispose itself for "the emancipation
of man," for the "right" to do wrong.

St. Ambrose's complete program of Christian civi-
lization is set forth in a work that is entitled (charac-
teristically enough) not *Rights* but *Duties*. The title of
De Officiis Ministrorum [26] (c.391) is in fact taken from
Cicero's great work on moral duty. The Doctor of the
Church keeps the style and most of the contents of the
Roman moralist. Nothing is lost and much is gained.
Roman self-control rises to the level of Christian
purity; Cicero's somewhat stilted and frigid account of
social well doing is illumined and warmed with the
Ambrosian passion for Christian charity.

And meanwhile Ambrose, the Governor-Bishop, the
administrator, the man of will, conscience, energy, action, is likewise a delicate poet and the writer of charming letters; and, above all, he is a tender pastor of souls.
He was, in a word, an integral humanist of whom
neither the Faith nor the Forum had need to be
ashamed.

[25] Migne, *Pat. Lat.*, xli (*De Civitate Dei*, V, 26).
[26] Migne, *Pat. Lat.*, xvi.

German Force and Celtic Fancy

The *Pax Romana,* the Latin order of material prosperity, did not endure. In 410, St. Augustine and St. Jerome wept over the sack of Rome by Alaric. In 476, with the deposition of Romulus Augustulus, complete collapse seemed inevitable. With the onslaughts of the Barbarians came a crucial test for Christian humanism. In the face of the crisis there were three possibilities. Some Christians might have been content to say their prayers, leaving the light of culture to flicker down and die. A few among the litterateurs kept their eyes turned longingly to the earlier and happier days and sang sad, futile songs in aristocratic and artistic isolation. Others looked bravely into the fierce, blue eyes of the tall barbarians, and asked themselves: What can be done to gain these, too, for the Kingdom of God? It was this last class that made the world safe for Christendom.

The collapse of Roman civilization was not as sudden or complete as it is sometimes represented. Disintegration proceeded gradually. Under the pagan Diocletian in the year 300, imperial power and organization were still intact; but the purely pagan Latin culture was finished. Even in 100 A.D., there was no heir either to Virgil (70 B.C.–19 B.C.), or to Cicero (106 B.C.–46 B.C.), or even to Ovid (43 B.C.–17 A.D.), or to Sallust (86 B.C.–34 B.C.). By 200, the wells of originality were dry; by 300, the future of Latin culture was in the hands of the Christians. In the course of the fourth and fifth centuries, the literary leadership of Ambrose and Jerome and Augustine and even of Cassian (360–435),

Rufinus (d.395), and Sulpicius Severus (360–432), touched the dead leaves of pagan literature with the magic of Christian inspiration, and flowers of extraordinary beauty blossomed forth. At least in regard to Latin letters, it cannot be said that the fall of Rome was due "to the disease of Christianity."

By 500, drastic changes had taken place. A "barbarian" Goth, Theodoric (493–526), ruled Italy in the place of the Western Emperor; while three Christian Romans were facing the cultural and religious problems of an age of transition. These were Boethius, Cassiodorus and Benedict; a speculative genius reflecting the *sophia* of the Greeks, a practical educator representing Roman *helikia,* a Saint whose thought and actions were inspired by the *charis* of Christ.

Boethius (c.475–525) came from a Roman family of consular rank. Educated in Greece, he returned to Rome and rose in favor with Theodoric. Later, accused of disloyalty, he was thrown into prison. While waiting for death, he reflected on the instability of a purely temporal happiness and wrote the *De Consolatione Philosophiae,* one of the sublimest of all pleas for the humanistic pursuit of happiness.

Cassiodorus (c.480–c.575), too, was a Roman. For three generations his family had held important posts in southern Italy. Like Boethius he won the favor of Theodoric. He retired from public life to a monastery, and there labored to harmonize the culture of Antiquity with that of Christendom.

The third of these Romans, St. Benedict (c.480–c.543), gave to the Middle Ages an organized monasticism that was destined to prove one of the greatest of all agents of culture and civilization. The three men taken together kept alive the ideals of speculation, education, sanctification; of Wisdom and Age and Grace.

By 600, the Middle Ages have definitely begun. The highest leadership of the West is in the hands of a Roman who is also a Saint, Pope Gregory the Great (590–604). The Papacy proved, in the crisis, to be the only center of unity that could hold world order together. Culture found its best home in Spain under Bishop Isidore of Seville (c.560–636), not a profound or original thinker, but a teacher willing to make the "Barbarians" his pupils.

By 700, the face of things is still more changed. Even the Papacy, under Sergius I (687–701), is no longer in a commanding position. But far up to the North, in England, a light was shining. Bede of Northumbria, a full-blooded "Barbarian," kindled the smoldering embers of learning into a bright flame. Taught by Benedict Biscop (c.628–690), who had been taught by Theodore of Tarsus (602–690), scholar and ecclesiastical statesman from far-off Asia Minor, Bede had a command of Latin, Greek and Hebrew. He spent a long life counting it "sweet to be ever learning or teaching or writing," and gave to the world (in addition to his homiletic and theological and purely literary works) an incomparable *Ecclesiastical History of the English People*.

By 800, the transition is over. With the coronation of Charlemagne we have the Holy Roman Empire that was to last (at least theoretically) for the next thousand years; and the "Carolingian Renaissance" under Alcuin (c.735–804), Einhard (c.770–840), and the rest. It is futile to ask whether this "Empire" or this "Renaissance" was "Roman" or "German." The fact is that civilization would no more have endured in a purely pagan Rome than culture could have flourished in a purely barbarian Germany. The Catholic Church saved Rome and gave the Germans culture and religion. In writing the *De Civitate Dei* after the "fall" of Rome in 410, Augustine had seen that the City of God would outlast that "fall"; and Salvian of Marseilles, with hardly less insight, saw in his *De Gubernatione Dei* that the Barbarians converted to Christendom were to be the ministers of Rome's salvation.

What saved both Rome and the Barbarians was the determination of Christian bishops. Men like Archbishop Avitus (c.490–518), a relative of the Emperor Avitus (466–56), went out to the Barbarians of Burgundy and kindled among them a flame of learning and piety. In the midst of exhaustive administrative work he found time to compose a long poem on the *Fall* (not of Rome but) *of Man*. It may contain plenty of poor Latin and worse poetry, but it taught the lesson of what Grace can do for human nature; and so long as that lesson is taught, the world is safe for both culture and civilization.

Bishop Remigius of Rheims (d.535) did for the Franks what Avitus did for the Burgundians. Clovis (d.511) was baptized in 496. Even a century later, Gregory of Tours (538–594) had trouble in mastering Latin; but his *Ecclesiastical History of the Franks*

(584) entitles its author to be called "The Herodotus of the Barbarians."

The tradition of Christian humanism incorporated, then, not only Greek thought and Roman Law, but also Barbarian force. It likewise found a place for Celtic fancy.

Celtic charm, like German vigor, might have been a danger. Canalized by logic, law and the Grace of God, it became a powerful element in Christian culture. Without Grace, all civilization in the long run degenerates. Without Redemption, seven capital sins rule the world. The Greek falls into pride; the Roman, into sensuality, greed, gluttony, lust; the Barbarians, into anger and envy; the Celt, into sloth. Happily, the harness of Grace can hold all these untamed tendencies together; and the synthesis of Grace with Hellenic wisdom, Roman efficiency, Teutonic fierceness and Celtic imagination makes for a richer humanism.

In a well-known essay,[27] Ernest Renan has given us an attractive, if somewhat imaginative picture of this imaginative people. He first pictures the Normans, plump and placid, with their amazing and Roman-like ability of assimilating whatever they found, whether in France, England, Italy or Russia; and then, by way of contrast, he presents Brittany with its charming, elf-like inhabitants. Of the Celtic character, he writes:

> it has all the failings and all the good qualities of the solitary man; at once proud and timid, strong in feel-

[27] "The Poetry of the Celtic Races," Harvard Classics, vol. 32, pp. 143-191.

ing and feeble in action; at home, freé and unreserved;
to the outside world, awkward and embarrassed. It
distrusts the foreigner, because it sees in him a being
more refined than itself, who abuses its simplicity.
Indifferent to the admiration of others, it asks only
one thing, that it should be left to itself.[28]

Renan divides Celtic literature into three completely
separate compartments: the epics of the early Bards,
the romances of a later period, and ecclesiastical writings. By innuendo, he suggests that the flower of Celtic
imaginative writing was all done prior to, or remote
from, the influence of Christianity, by Celtic Bards un-
sullied by the taint of Christian monachism. The reality
was somewhat different. Caesar and Tacitus were able
to give a favorable picture of the Germans: that of the
pre-Christian Celts was far from flattering. The Teutonic tribes appear to have been tame in comparison
with the wild, blood-thirsty Celts. When the Irishman
comes into literary history, he is already Christianized.
There was in reality no divorce between secular and
ecclesiastical writings—all three types were in fact
written by the same "Gray men of the Monasteries."
The Legend of St. Brendan is typical of the Christianized fancy of the Celts. In his voyage to the Land of
Promise, on a rock in the Polar Seas, Brendan sees
Judas enjoying a weekly holiday from Hell, by reason
of an act of charity he once performed. This sort of
imagination, compact of human tenderness and sym-
pathy is a new note possible only in Christian culture.

Yet, even before they were Christianized, the Celts

[28] *Op. cit.*, p. 146.

had a belief in the immortality of the soul; and the Celtic love of mystery easily led to exalted heights of Christian devotion. So that St. Patrick (c.389–461), a Celt trained in Roman schools, was able to win them to the Faith, unite the unruly clans and give some order to the land. From his death in 461 to the coming of the Danes, there was in Ireland a Golden Age of Christian culture. As early as the sixth century, when Benedict, Boethius and Cassiodorus were the lone leaders of thought in Europe, there was in Ireland an upsurge of intellectual life, with great monastic schools to which thousands of students flocked. They eagerly learned the Latin language which seemed so much sweeter than their own, and which gave them access to treasures of an older civilization.

Renan admits the spiritual influence of the Irish monasteries: "Nowhere, perhaps, has God been better worshipped in spirit then in these great monastic communities of Hy, or of Iona, of Bangor, of Clonard, or of Lindisfarne." [29] Celtic humanists carried the treasures of their learning and the charm of their imagination throughout Europe. An Irish monk, far from home, will lay aside his Aristotle, and write in the margin of a book lines like these on his pussy, Pangur Bán.

> I and Pangur Bán, my cat,
> 'Tis a like task we are at;
> Hunting mice is his delight,
> Hunting words I sit all night.
> Oftentimes a mouse will stray
> In the hero Pangur's way;

[29] *Op. cit.,* p. 180.

Oftentimes my keen thought set
Takes a meaning in its net.
'Gainst the wall he sets his eye
Full and fierce and sharp and sly;
'Gainst the wall of knowledge I
All my little wisdom try.
When a mouse darts from its den,
O how glad is Pangur then!
O what gladness do I prove
When I solve the doubts I love!
So in peace our tasks we ply,
Pangur Bán, my cat and I;
In our arts we find our bliss,
I have mine and he has his.[30]

No Greek could have written that. It is indicative of the new kind of charm which had come into Christian culture and was spreading throughout Europe. Not, however, that the Irish mind was incapable of hard thinking. To quote Renan again:

The Celtic character after having put in practice all chivalries, devout and worldly, gone with Peredur in quest of the Holy Grail and fair ladies and dreamed with St. Brendan of mystical Atlantides, who knows what it would produce in the domain of intellect if it hardened itself to an entrance into the world and subjected its rich and profound nature to the conditions of modern thought? [31]

The flourishing of great schools in the British Isles and on the Continent did in fact produce such scholars

[30] Robin Flower, *Poems and Translations* (N. Y., 1931), p. 129.
[31] *Op. cit.,* p. 190.

as Columbanus (543–615), Alcuin and John Scotus
Erigena (c.810–c.880).

Imagination, humor, delicate sentiment, élan of the
spirit, otherworldliness, the ideal of chivalry, and subtle thinking—all these and much more enriched Christian humanism after the conversion of Ireland to
Christianity.

CHAPTER III

LIGHT IN THE DARK AGES

THE idea of *the* Renaissance is largely a myth—the creation of modern writers since about 1840. Certainly, not even the humanists who lived during the fifteenth century ever spoke of participating in a Renaissance of culture.

Burckhardt (1818–1897) and Symonds (1840–1893), in their works[1] on the so-called Renaissance, showed few qualms of conscience; but the Italian Bartoli (1833–1894), in his *Precursors of the Renaissance,* began to suspect the truth, namely, that humanism did not have to be reborn, but only revived. Christian culture has never died. It needs only the fertile soil of encouragement and an atmosphere of peace to cause it to blossom into beauty. *Sapientia revirescens,* cultural second spring, was already spoken of by Lupus of Ferrières in the ninth century.

THE CAROLINGIAN REVIRESCENCE

Charlemagne provided the necessary conditions for a revival of learning. Culture, to a great extent, de-

[1] Jacob Burckhardt, *The Civilization of the Renaissance in Italy* (trans. by S. G. C. Middlemore) ; John Addington Symonds, *Renaissance in Italy.*

pends upon peace; if its roots are embedded in the past, it will flourish under the right political conditions. Charlemagne created such an atmosphere; and between the years 790 and 890, an enthusiasm for learning swept over the Empire.

Up in Britain, there was Alcuin, a typical product of the British schools. Steeped in the tradition of Theodore of Tarsus, Benedict Biscop and Bede, Alcuin came to the court of Charlemagne. If there had been no Charlemagne, Alcuin might have remained an obscure school teacher in York. But at imperial Aix-la-Chapelle, wide horizons opened to him and the whole Empire acclaimed him as a master. He was not an original thinker; but rather a teacher who inspired his pupils with a passionate ardor for learning. His remarkable verse reveals a wide acquaintance with classical poets like Virgil, Ovid, Lucan, Statius and Horace, as well as with Christian writers like Orosius, Augustine and Salvian.

Learning flourished wherever this was possible at this period. Even Charlemagne, we are told, understood Latin fairly well, and had a smattering of Greek. He had a special love for Augustine's *City of God*. His outlook was continental. Hearing of Peter of Pisa, a brilliant Italian scholar versed in Greek, he endowed him with a scholarship and brought him to Aix. From the north of Italy, Paul the Deacon (c.720–c.800) was summoned, having attracted the attention of the emperor by his knowledge of Augustine. Paul shed light on his age by writing a *History of the Lombards* and a *Life of Gregory the Great*. These teachers proposed to

Charlemagne a law that might aid in fostering culture. So, in 782, there was issued what has been termed the "Charter of Modern Thought," addressed to bishops and abbots, admonishing them to be zealous for the study of letters as well as for regularity of life in their monasteries.[2] Later, decrees were issued penalizing those who held positions of trust without adequate knowledge.

In Spain, a Goth attracted attention—Theodulphus (d.821), Latinist, poet, theologian and bishop. This was the marvel of these ninth-century humanists: they were scholars, poets, law makers, statesmen, traveled men of the world, and yet pious enough to be made bishops—men who, wherever they went, if they did not find a school, founded one.

The court of Charlemagne would have been incomplete without some Irishmen, the *Hibernici exules,* who were disseminating their learning through Europe. Charlemagne held them in special esteem. Clement, the Irishman, who called himself "a vendor of learning," spent some months at the court at Aix where he gained a great reputation and "planted the mustard seed that developed into the tree of learning at Paris." Dungal (fl.810–825), the Irish monk, after visiting Charlemagne, founded a school at Pavia, destined to develop into one of the great centers of learning in the fifteenth century. Donatus (d.876), an Irish teacher, poet and Bishop of Fiesole, like his two predecessors, taught

[2] See J. B. Mullinger, *Schools of Charles the Great* (New York, 1911), p. 101.

Greek, wrote good prose and poetry, contributing greatly to the revival of learning.

One of the best Latin prose writers of the age was Einhard, of whom W. P. Ker, in *The Dark Ages,* has said that "he was more classical than the classical writers he imitated." He was more classical than the correct Suetonius because he had far more life and more seriousness of purpose. Einhard, the Frank, trained at Fulda and sent to the court of Charlemagne, was a layman, an architect by profession, a classical scholar by disposition, and a pious man by instinct.

Of recent date, historians are emphasizing how extensive was the culture that illumined Europe during the ninth century. Rabanus Maurus (c.776–856) founded a school at Fulda on the frontier of Saxony, and dedicated his life to teaching. The most learned man of his times, he had been a disciple of Alcuin at Tours; later, he returned to advance the spiritual, intellectual and temporal welfare of his monastery. Besides being conversant with all sacred and profane learning, he wrote verse and books on the theory of teaching.

One of his disciples was Servatus Lupus who became Abbot of Ferrières. He was one of the most cultured men of his day. He knew everyone of note in Europe, as is testified by his 130 letters, all distinguished by literary elegance. These letters are illuminating in their revelation of the genuine culture of these scholars. Quietly, they were doing much that modern scholars are now attempting. In one letter, we see his eagerness to track down a reference to Cicero in different manuscripts; in another, he compares the merits of Cicero and Quintilian; in a third, he mentions a manuscript at Tours and decides to send someone to copy it. All is not smooth sailing, however, for these humanists. In letter 34, Lupus betrays his depression over the defeat of culture; in a later letter, courage has revived, revealing his hopes of a revirescence of culture, *sapientia revirescens*.

Walafrid Strabo (809–849), disciple of Rabanus Maurus, preceptor at the court of Charlemagne's grandson, Charles the Bald, also spread humanism by his hymns and verses in fluent, elegant Latin. The Benedictine Abbot of Corbie, Paschasius Radbertus (c.790–865), has left writings, not only steeped in the early Fathers of the Church, but abounding in classical allusions.

Among the Irish humanists, the greatest was John Scotus Erigena (c.810–c.875), whose universal scholarship and subtle mind attracted the attention of the whole Empire. Down in Italy, the Pope's secretary, Anastasius Bibliothecarius, expresses his surprise that a "Barbarian" should know Greek and be able to write Latin poems and a treatise on mystical theology.

After the death of Charlemagne and the dismemberment of his Empire, education received a setback, except for a brief period under Charles the Bald. Soon other cares and problems possessed the minds of rulers. But new seeds of humanism had been sown; the monasteries, seats of learning, continued to flourish. The roots of Christian culture were not destroyed even amid the terrorism of a new barbarian invasion.

The British Isles

To speak of Anglo-Saxon culture is somewhat misleading; the early literature of England was less Teutonic in its inspiration than Roman and Catholic. Many authors, of course, claim the opposite. Thus, Professor A. R. Waller writes: "English literature, as we know it, arose from the spirit inherent in the Viking makers of England before they finally settled in this island." [3] Professor H. Munro Chadwick states: "The poetry of the Old English period is generally grouped in two main divisions, national and Christian. To the former are assigned those poems of which the subjects are drawn from English or rather Teutonic tradition and history or from the customs and conditions of English life." [4] Both these statements, at least in their implications, are incorrect.

For five hundred years before the arrival of the Anglo-Saxons, Britain had enjoyed a rich culture and civilization. From the coming of Julius Caesar in 55 B.C., to the withdrawal of the Roman legions in 410 A.D., the Celtic tribes of Britain had assimilated much that their Roman masters had to teach them. Roman roads, fortifications, villas and baths made of the island a Roman province. All this gave impetus to contacts, exchange of ideas, the use of Latin as a

[3] *Cambridge History of English Literature* (N. Y., 1933), vol. I, p. 1.
[4] *Ibid.*, p. 21.

national language and, finally, to a fairly complete Romanized culture.

Moreover, for five hundred years before this Roman conquest, a Celtic culture had existed. Thus, for a thousand years, the natives of Britain had known much of poetry, law, wisdom and organization. At the end of this period, they could hardly have become so lazy as to allow their culture to crumble away completely. The truth seems to be that the Anglo-Saxons, by the force of superior physical strength, overcame the Romanized Celts, gradually took possession of their land, imposed their language, submerged and made inarticulate a cultured people with a long tradition.

From 450 to 600, darkness reigned. Only two books are left of those which are known to deal with this night of British civilization: *De Excidio Britanniae* by Gildas, a Welshman or Breton, describing the conditions of England in the sixth century and the *Historia Britonum* by Nennius, who flourished about 800. From their victims, who were men of ideas, and of energy that showed itself in Roman ways of ploughing, building, sewing, and the rest, the invaders had much to learn. Twenty years before the Angles had come to England, St. Germanus (d.448), Bishop of Auxerre, had been there, debating with the natives the subtlest points of Augustinian theology.

In 597, when Pope Gregory sent St. Augustine as chaplain to Queen Bertha, England returned to the culture of Europe. Laws began to be written; old customs were revised. Poetry, sermons, art and organization came to life. Obediently, the Angles and Saxons received Christian ideals from St. Augustine. He found some churches and manor houses but little else that remained of Roman civilization. When he penetrated farther west, however, and talked with a group of the British clergy, he was amazed at their learning. Had they not lost their tempers at his apparent Roman pompousness, the Saint might even have learned and taught in their language.

There was, then, no purely Anglo-Saxon culture; it was rather an aggregate tradition with Celtic, Roman and Anglo-Saxon elements, all taken over and inspired by Christianity.

As for "National" Anglo-Saxon poetry—there is none outside the Christian tradition. *Beowulf* is not a pagan poem; it is the creation of a Christian, possibly of a monk. The legends had come from Denmark and Sweden, but the Norsemen knew comparatively little of composition or literary creation. By the eighth century, these legends had become grist for the Christian poet's mill. They were welded together into a single allegorical song intimating the Divine Mystery of Redemption—a conception beyond the scope of a Viking's power.

The story of *Beowulf* opens with a legend of the sea-burial of King Scyld Scefing, founder of the Scylding dynasty. A genealogy of Danish Kings follows up to Hrothgar; and we are taken to his great Mead-Hall, Heorot, which reveals elements of Roman civilization. Here we have the story of the Monster Grendel (descendant of the Biblical Cain, the first murderer), who nightly devoured the thanes of King Hrothgar.

Beowulf, son of Ecgtheow and nephew of King
Hygelac, comes to aid in overcoming Grendel. After
Beowulf's victory over Grendel, in which he wrenched
off one arm, King Hrothgar celebrates with a banquet.
The Christian allegory behind this legend is evident
enough: Grendel is the Devil; Beowulf, offering himself for others, is Christ redeeming man by self-
sacrifice. Celtic imagination is displayed in the story
of the slaying, by Beowulf, of Grendel's mother in her
lair, a cave at the bottom of a pool. After this feat,
Beowulf swims to the surface in his armor, the sword-
hilt in one hand and the head of the monster in the
other. A Christian sermon on pride lasts through one
hundred lines. The author, to round out the epic struc-
ture, takes us to the land of the Geats, which Hygelac
is ruling and where Beowulf eventually becomes King.
After fifty years of wise rule, the hero signalizes himself in a victory-in-death over the Fire Dragon. The
suggestion throughout the epic is that evil exists, and
that man falls and needs a Saviour who will redeem
him by the conquest of evil.

The interpretation of this poem which makes it a
Nordic creation with a veneer of Christianity added at
a later date can no longer be maintained. The only
manuscript of *Beowulf* dates from around 1000 A.D.;
but the poem was written in the age of Bede about the
year 700. Throughout it there are echoes of Virgil,
St. Paul and St. Augustine; there are no praises of
pagan worship. The civilization depicted is Christian
with Roman touches. The work is that of a writer
who had assimilated all the Nordic legends and had

reformed them into a Christian epic, full of action and imagination, one purpose of which was clearly to edify the Christians of his age.

Other shorter poems of this period, usually attributed to Anglo-Saxon origin, can also be traced to European influence; although, because much of this poetry treats of nature and the sea, some scholars have concluded that they were the creations of Anglo-Saxon genius. It is only too well known that sailors no more love the the sea in a literary way than the farmers delight in nature. *The Seafarer* and *The Wanderer* are products of a literary love of the sea tinged with a Christian nostalgia for heaven. Cynewulf, possibly the Bishop of Lindisfarne (d.787), was a poet of this type—as monkish as a man could be, yet with a "pagan" love for nature, sea and battle. What little was known of him shows him to be a man of great education. His Celtic strain comes out in more than one element of his writings. A monk, his thought was always of Christ. In a language like that of *Beowulf,* he has given us in his beautiful poem, *The Christ,* the story of Our Saviour's Life and Second Coming.

What is true of Anglo-Saxon poetry is even more true of the Latin literature written in England. One of the earliest Latinists is Gildas (516–570), "the wisest of the Britons" as Alcuin calls him. In his *De Excidio et Conquestu Britanniae,* written about 547, he refers to Latin as "our language." In this narrative, he describes "The fierce and impious Saxons, a race hateful to God and man—a wolfish offspring." He also castigates the British, "with whom," he says, "it has always been a custom to be impotent in repelling foreign foes, but bold and invincible in raising civil war." Gildas, in using Latin, expresses his conviction that he was a citizen of Christendom. The same reason impelled St. Patrick to write his *Confessions* in Latin.

From the sixth to the ninth century, England gloried in a series of scholarly teachers. Theodore of Tarsus (602–690), one of the best the northern world had known, settled at Canterbury in 668. Classical to his fingertips, he brought with him all the traditions of Greek learning. He initiated the youth of Britain into the beauties of Homer; and soon they were as versed in Greek and Latin as in their mother-speech. With his congenial companion, Hadrian, he labored fruitfully in making learning and sanctity flourish throughout England.

One of the most scholarly disciples of these great teachers was Aldhelm (639–709),[5] an "Englishman" of varied accomplishments: poet, musician, linguist, who, besides knowing Latin and Hebrew, was said "to have pronounced Greek like the Greek natives." William of Malmesbury (d.1143), says that he so fully imbibed the liberal arts that he was wonderful in each of them and unrivaled in all. For the learned nuns of the time, he wrote two works: one in prose, *De Laudibus Virginitatis,* and one in hexameters, *De Laude Virginum*. This cultured scholar was European in his training, steeped in the tradition of Virgil, Augustine and Isidore; he was Celtic in his romantic imagery.

[5] *Dictionary of National Biography,* i, 245.

In the case of Venerable Bede (674–735),[6] his all-embracing humanism can only be explained by the fact that he received his culture from Europe. Music, mathematics, rhetoric, medicine, Greek, Hebrew, Latin, Scripture and theology were among his attainments. He had a passion for history and he went to extreme lengths to verify facts for his great work, *Historia Ecclesiastica Gentis Anglorum.* Without this monumental work, we would know scarcely anything about the Anglo-Saxons. The historian, Charles Plummer, editing the *Opera* of Bede, traces the origin of his erudition to Caesar, Orosius, Gildas, Gregory, and others.

The Vikings' spirit could contribute little to this Golden Age of Christian scholarship. Gregorian music, architecture, glassmaking, art, philosophy, letters and calligraphy, these we owe to cultured Christian monks.

NORMAN CULTURE

During the latter part of the eighth and the ninth centuries, marauding seafarers began a series of activities that horrified not only England but France, Spain and the lower Rhine country. The piratical descents of the Barbarians upon Britain in the middle of the fifth century pale in comparison with these later onslaughts. In 787, an attack was begun on Wessex. Swift destruction of the monasteries of Northumbria followed. By 795, Scotland, Ireland and Wales were invaded. These Northmen accomplished astonishing exploits: they established towns in Ireland; seized most of the Scot-

[6] *Op. cit.,* iv, 98.

tish Islands; in 863, founded at Novgorod and Kiev a Russian state; in 874, colonized Iceland, and, in 983, Greenland; in 880, attacked Austrasia (Belgium and the cities of the lower Rhine); in 911, received the Duchy of Normandy; won nearly all England (987-1016); discovered "Vinland" in America, about 1000; in 1020, landed in lower Italy, receiving the Duchy of Apulia in 1055; and in 1097, they helped to win the First Crusade.

Once these buccaneers were settled, however, they accepted the Christian Faith and European civilization. Their success was due, mainly, to sheer energy and enterprising leadership. Rurik in Russia, Olaf Tryggvason in Norway, Cnut in Denmark, and Rollo in Normandy possessed political ability of a high order.

Vladimir the Great, Grand Duke of Kiev, Novgorod and all Russia, decided the destiny of Russia when he embraced Christianity in 988 and delivered his country into the keeping of the Patriarch of Constantinople. In the same year, he sent the Varangian Guard, made up of six thousand Scandinavians, to aid the Byzantine Emperor against the Greeks. In Italy the Normans moved north from Sicily, ravaging and conquering. They defeated the Pope in warfare, at Civitella, 1053; yet were defeated in turn by a stroke of diplomacy. Recognizing their skill and adventurous spirit, Pope Urban II enlisted them in the First Crusade.

In 911, Charles the Simple, King of the West Franks, ceded Normandy to Rollo as a fief. The leader took his new position seriously. He rebuilt and re-endowed the abbeys pillaged by his countrymen. By degrees, Christianity became the adopted religion of this duchy; the laws of Normandy became Frankish and the speech became French.

Two examples may serve to illustrate "Norman culture." Lanfranc (1005–1089),[7] born in Pavia, Italy, of combined Teutonic and Latin ancestry, trained by a liberal education, taught law with marked success, and then sought further education in the great schools of France. In 1046, he reached Normandy and entered the monastery of Bec; shortly after, he became prior and opened a school which attracted scholars from all over Europe. Several of these pupils rose to positions of high rank; among them, Pope Alexander II and Saint Anselm.

In 1050, Lanfranc attended the council of Rome to oppose the heresies of Berengarius of Tours (998–1088), who had gone astray on the doctrine of the Blessed Sacrament. Appointed to the abbacy of St. Stephen's at Caen in 1066, Lanfranc became Archbishop of Canterbury in 1070. An Italian, fluent in French and Latin, Lanfranc mingled with the Anglo-Saxons, and became a pillar of the Norman Church. As scholar, author, statesman and ecclesiastic, he exhibited sound sense, rare tact and singular ability. For seventeen years, he wielded an influence throughout Norman England second only to the King's.

There was the same blending of statesmanship, sanctity and culture in St. Anselm (1033–1109),[8] a

[7] *Op. cit.*, xxxii, 83.

[8] *Saint Anselm, a Critical Biography,* by Joseph Clayton (Milwaukee, 1933).

theologian, statesman, classical scholar, distinguished
writer, and poet of a high order. He was, *par excellence,*
a fulfillment of the vocation to advance in wisdom, age
and grace before God and man. Born at Aosta, in Italy,
amid distinctions of all kinds (the baronial palace of his
father was a seat of chivalry and Christian culture), he
was fired at an early age with a love of learning. He
crossed the Alps into France, and entered the Abbey
of Bec, where he became Lanfranc's most gifted pupil.
As prior of Bec, he wrote his famous *Monologion.* The
Greek title (meaning a single reason or argument for
the existence of God) is significant. The southern
Normans knew Greek; the northerners were curious
about it: an indication of the growing influence of the
classical tradition. In this treatise, Anselm set forth his
a priori proof of the existence of God. The *Proslogion*
which followed was likewise concerned with the existence of God. These writings marked the beginnings of
Scholasticism. "Faith seeking to be understood" *(fides
quaerens intellectum)* embodied its essence; "I believe
in order that I may understand" *(credo ut intelligam)*
was its working principle.

Abbot of Bec in 1078, Anselm was destined to suc-
ceed Lanfranc in the see of Canterbury. At the Council
at Bari in Southern Italy, in 1098, Anselm was one of
the most distinguished theologians summoned to deal
with the difficulties raised by the Greeks in regard to the
"procession of the Holy Ghost." After this intellectual
debate, he returned to the thorny difficulty of lay in-
vestiture at home. The problem of Church and State in
England came to a crisis under William Rufus (1087–
1100). Anselm perceived clearly the distinction between

civil and ecclesiastical jurisdictions. His solution was simple: the Pope should present the crosier and, if a single person were both bishop and baron, the king should present the sword.

The next king, Henry I (1100–1135), called *Beauclerc* because of his finished scholarship, belonged to a different tradition from that of his elder brother, Rufus. Prince, knight, hunter, fencer, he was interested in ideas, music, architecture, and was responsible for much of the Gothic beauty that still remains in England. He was a man, too, of deep emotions. His range of thought and experience contributed to make his reign significant. Permanency was ensured to William the Conqueror's creation—the new kingdom of England; and two generations after the death of Anselm we shall find in England a new "race," resulting from the intermarriage of stolid Anglo-Saxons and cultured Normans.

Typical of this union was the scholar, Lawrence (d.1154),[9] a humanist teacher in the Cathedral School of Durham. Far from the intrigues of London, heedless of the baronial wars that characterized the reign of Stephen, this Benedictine prior, a classical scholar to his finger tips, was also a lawyer, an orator and a theologian, *juris peritus, eloquentia praeditus, divinis institutis sufficienter instructus.* His poems testify to his familiarity with Plautus, Cicero, Virgil, Ovid, Seneca and Lucan. His imitations of Horace, almost unparalleled in smoothness and perfection in the twelfth century, prove him to have been a man of very extraordinary taste. *Hypognosticon sive Memoriale veteris*

[9] *Dict. Nat. Biog.*, xxxii, 128.

et novi testamenti (on the hidden meaning of the Scriptures), a poem in nine books, is written in excellent, musical and vigorous verse.

Another Anglo-Norman scholar of this type was Robert Wace of Jersey, who flourished about 1150. Educated at Caen, he composed narrative poems in Norman-French. He was a pioneer in taking literature from the professors and offering it to the people. His *Roman de Brut,* a free paraphrase of Geoffrey of Monmouth, was popular with the people and added to a growing interest in the Arthurian tales. Wace's reputation, however, rests mainly on his *Roman de Rou* (Rollo).

Elsewhere, Norman poets were singing songs in their gay, new language. The Christian humanists were preparing a new "Renaissance."

CHAPTER IV

MEDIEVAL HUMANISM

BEFORE speaking of what is now frequently described as the Renaissance of the twelfth century, it is well to retrace our steps to say a word about those school-teachers (some of them quite obscure) to whose patient work under great difficulties medieval humanism owes so much. Even in the centuries when kings were unable to give peace and bishops too busy to set down written laws, the light of learning was not wholly extinguished.

The tradition of teaching is an old one, and does not easily die. Far outside the limits of Greek and Roman influence, Julius Caesar found Druids in Gaul; and "to these (he tells us) large numbers of young men resort for the purpose of instruction, and the Druids are in great honor among them." [1]

MONASTIC TEACHERS

Bede's account of the great Theodore and Hadrian has become classical:

> And for as much as both of them were, as has been said before, well read both in sacred and in secular literature, they gathered a crowd of disciples, and there

[1] *De Bello Gallico,* VI, 13.

daily flowed from them rivers of knowledge to water the hearts of their hearers; and, together with the books of Holy Writ, they also taught them the arts of ecclesiastical poetry, astronomy and arithmetic. A testimony of which is, there are still living at this day some of their scholars, who are as well versed in the Greek and Latin tongues as in their own, in which they were born. Nor were there ever happier times since the English came unto Britain; for their kings, being brave men and good Christians, they were a terror to all barbarous nations, and the minds of all men were bent upon the joys of the heavenly kingdom of which they had just heard; and all who desired to be instructed in sacred reading had masters at hand to teach them.

The teachers of the school of York, according to Alcuin, gathered a library that contained the best of the Patristic writings, of classical Latin prose and of all that Greece had given to Rome, the divinely inspired Scriptures of the Hebrews and the products of African scholarship (that is, the writings of St. Augustine and others). Alcuin mentions the authors by name. Among prose writers he mentions Jerome, Hilary, Ambrose, Augustine, Athanasius, Orosius, Victorinus and Boethius; Gregory and Leo; Basil and Chrysostom; Cassiodorus and Fulgentius; Aldhelm and Bede. Among earlier authors in prose or verse, he sites Pompeius (Trogus) and Pliny, Aristotle (doubtless in Latin) and Cicero, Virgil, Lucan and Statius; among later poets, Sedulius and Juvencus; among grammarians, Donatus and Priscian. The teachers who were familiar with such works may not have had the specialized skills of their modern successors; but it is difficult to deny the breadth of their humanistic outlook. They pursued both secular and religious learning; their two words *disciplina* and *custodia* covered many intellectual and moral virtues; the liberal arts went hand in hand with purity of life; they sought for a synthesis of Grace with nature, sanctity with song.

At the beginning of the "Dark Ages" there were schools and teachers in many parts of Europe, at Chartres, Tours, Rheims, Auxerre, St. Gall, Fulda, Reichenau, Maintz, Gandersheim, Solenhofen, Pavia and elsewhere. Distinguished teachers were connected with these schools: Rabanus Maurus (c.776–856), the pupil of Alcuin; Walafrid Strabo (d.849), Abbot of Reichenau, who had a genuine gift for poetry and became the tutor of Charles the Bald; Lupus Abbot of Ferrières, whose letters reveal his familiarity with Livy, Sallust, Caesar, Suetonius, Cicero, Quintilian, Terence, Virgil, Horace, and Martial among others; Rudolph, biographer of Rabanus Maurus; Paschasius Radbertus (790–865), Abbot of Old Corbie, near Amiens; Notker of St. Gall (c.950–1022); Eric of Auxerre (841–877), who knew Greek, and his distinguished pupil Remy (d.908); and John Scotus Erigena (c.810–c.880).

It is not wholly true to speak of the tenth century as the nadir of intellectual life. It is true that around the year 950 the number of teachers was comparatively small. Yet two famous teachers illumine even the darkest part of the "Dark Ages," Bruno of Cologne (925–965), and Gerbert of Aurillac (950–1003), one of the foremost scholars of his age. Gerbert taught at Tours,

Fleury, Sens and Rheims, became Archbishop of Ravenna and finally Pope (Silvester II) in 999. Although he describes his age as *dira et miseranda tempora,* it was in the schools of this same century that he acquired his learning. His pupil, Richer (fl.c.1000), in his history, has described the enthusiasm excited by Gerbert's lectures and the tide of scholars that flocked to him from all over France, Germany, Italy, and the British Islands. Prelates and princes glorified in having called him master: Fulbert of Chartres, Robert, King of France, the most religious and learned sovereign of his age, Otto of Germany (980–1002), and others.

Bruno (925–965) was a younger brother of Otto the Great. At Utrecht, under the Abbot Baldric, Bruno made rapid progress in Greek and Latin literature. Later he founded a Palatine School, on the model of that of Charlemagne, and taught the full curriculum of the liberal arts. Even when he became Archbishop of Cologne in 953, his interest in learning did not cease.

Meanwhile, in far-away Saxony, in the convent of Gandersheim a simple nun, Hrotswitha (932–c.1002), carried on the tradition of Christian humanism. In the very year (932) when the son of that awful woman Marozia was thrust on to the Papal throne and when wild hordes of Wends and Huns were destroying all they could reach, the little girl Hrotswitha came into the world. She entered the convent under the Abbess Berberga, niece of the Emperor Otto and, gathering together a shelf of books, she steeped herself in Latin literature. One day she brought to the Abbess a sheaf of verse, conceived in the half serious, half humorous

mood that has ever been the note of humanistic culture,
and containing lines like these:

> *Hanc quoque sordidulam tenta purgare Camenam*
> *Ac fulcire tui flore magisterii.*

> Try, if thou canst, my sooty Muse to clean
> And let my lisping on thy learning lean.

A later poem on a Christian boy, martyred by the Mos-
lems in Spain, contains verse that is nothing short of
remarkable. Take the point in the poem where the
Moorish King is mauling and pampering the lad to no
good purpose. The little fellow reacts by punching the
brute on the nose. The following translation into English can do more than hint at the movement of Hrotswitha's vivid Latin:

> Then he up with a swing, and he cudgeled the king
> With blows to his eyes and his nose,
> Till his tangled beard was sore clotted, and smeared
> Were the garments he wore with gore.

Let anyone who knows Latin read the lines aloud:

> *Osque petit subito pugno regale vibrato,*
> *Intulit et tantum pronis obtutibus ictum*
> *Sanguis ut absque mora, stillans de vulnere facto,*
> *Barbam foedavit, nec non vestes madefecit.*

You can see and hear the punch in the swift dactyls of
the first line; and then the slow spondees that follow
make you fairly feel the oozy mess of blood that trickles
through the Moorish beard and makes his cloak all
clammy.

There is one line of Hrotswitha that I am very fond

of. It occurs in a poem in which Theophilus (anticipating Goethe's *Faust*) makes a contract with the Devil. Only, in Hrotswitha's poem, the Blessed Virgin snatches the document from the Devil's hand; and so Theophilus, who was spiritually dead, through that dear Lady, began once more to live. I like to apply the line to Catholic humanism. Through Hrotswitha, it too came back to life after it had seemed, for a moment, dead.

Sed postquam periit, per te, sacra Virgo, revixit.

The eleventh century ushered in a new period of intellectual progress. The outstanding teacher of this age was Fulbert of Chartres (960–1028). He was important politically and ecclesiastically as well as intellectually. The pupil of Gerbert, in his own turn, he became preceptor to many men of letters who distinguished themselves in France during the eleventh century. The Latin verses of Adelman of Liége, his pupil, which by accident have come down to us, are doubtless only one of many eulogies about the great Fulbert. They do credit to both the pupil and the teacher. One has only to read aloud lines like the following to realize what new wine of music the eleventh century could put into the old bottles of Latin words.

> *Dum te conor dicere*
> *Sermo fugit, cor liquescit,*
> *Recrudescunt lacrimae.*

> When I try to sing of thee
> Language falters, feelings fill me,
> And my eyes break out in tears.

Such verse, unlike classical Latin, is wholly accentual; and that, of course, heightens its singing quality. Even the youngsters in their early teens seem to have delighted in the lilt of accented Latin verse. Among the happy survivals of that age there is a metrical letter written by two brothers, Arnaud and Jacques, in which they tell their mother, who happened to be called Joy, that they were hard up and badly in need of cash.

> *Mater nostra,*
> *Mater grata,*
>   *Nomine Laetitia,*
> *Nomen tuum*
> *Nomen laetum*
>   *Praebet nobis gaudia.*
> *Mater opem*
> *Nunc praesentem*
>   *Fer utrique filio;*
> *Tuo namque*
> *Nunc uterque*
>   *Indiget auxilio.*

Mother, dear one
Mother, loved one,
  By thy name, Felicitous,

A name of Joy
Without alloy,
  A very source of joy to us!

Right away
Without delay,
  Mother, to the rescue go!

We're just about
Down and out,
  And terribly in need of dough.

Of course we can assume that the master was at the elbow of the boys. But this little poem, so full of human nature, surely tells us a great deal of what was going on in all the schools of Europe. The tradition of culture was safe with boys like Arnaud and Jacques (and their school teacher) even in the "Dark Ages."

THE TWELFTH CENTURY

Until recently, the twelfth was the Cinderella of the centuries. Long after the thirteenth had been "rediscovered," the twelfth remained unappreciated. The history of culture during this time includes the complete development of Romanesque art and the rise of Gothic, the full bloom of vernacular poetry (both lyric and epic) the new learning and new literature in Latin, the beginnings of university foundations in Salerno, Bologna, Paris, Montpellier and Oxford, the additions to the educational program of Roman and Canon Law, the new Aristotle, the new Euclid and Ptolemy, and the works of Greek and Arab physicians; the revival of the Latin classics, prose and verse, both in the ancient style and in the new rhythms of the Goliardi; the formation of the liturgical drama; new varieties of historical writing; the beginnings of a new science; developments in philosophy; and much else.

It was not because the scholars of the twelfth century went back to the classics that they became humanists; rather, because they were fundamentally humanistic in inclination, they desired both to create new forms of literature in the vernacular and to imitate the classics, to translate the treasures from the Greek and

Arab world and to indulge in humor in the new, gay Goliardic way; to push back the borders of their ignorance by adding to their knowledge of philosophy and medicine; to satisfy their imaginations by new forms of architecture. It was a rich and varied century, a converging point for the many rays of thought and culture that had penetrated singly through the preceding centuries.

From many centers of learning the light of humanism radiated all over Europe.[2] The teachers were the recognized aristocrats of the mind. Benedictine monasteries played a varied and important role. To quote C. H. Haskins: "A monastery might be a refuge for travelers, an economic centre, a lamp of architecture, an exchange of ideas and information, a source of new types in music and literature." One of these great centers was Monte Cassino, which boasts a long line of illustrious men beginning with St. Benedict (d.543), and including Peter the Deacon (1107–1153), Constantine the African, called a "new and shining Hippocrates," Alfano of Salerno, and Alberic the Rhetorician (fl.1080). Perhaps the most famous intellectual center of the time was Bec, in Normandy, made famous by Lanfranc, Anselm, Pope Alexander II and a great number of bishops and abbots. Across the channel, the intellectual life of England flowered in the abbey of Westminster which had inherited its traditions from

[2] Much of what is here told briefly is set forth in much detail in *The Renaissance of the Twelfth Century*, by C. H. Haskins (Cambridge, Massachusetts, 1927); and this work, in turn, is largely a summary of many works that have appeared in the last twenty-five years.

Bec. In Spain the Arabs had been pushed back and new schools of learning sprang up along the pilgrim routes. Toledo became the center of the amalgamated culture of Moors and Christians.

The twelfth century also saw the rise or flourishing of new religious Orders: the Carthusians (1084), the Premonstratensians (1124), the Orders of Grammont (1076), Fontevrault (1100). The purpose of many of these was spiritual rather than intellectual; yet, these new Orders furthered the intellectual history of the age by counteracting the localism of many individual monasteries. They fostered regular communication between different and often widely distant establishments. Monastic travel to and from Rome and pilgrimages to Jerusalem and Compostela were encouraged. Hostels for travelers and shrines of devotion collected and passed on the rich material for the epics and *Chansons de gestes* that grew around these pilgrimages.

As there are no frontiers of the mind, all the scholars of Europe exchanged ideas in the universal language of Rome. The age teemed with great writers and teachers: Hildebert of Lavardin (1056–1133), at Le Mans and Tours; Gilbert de la Porrée (1080–1154), at Poitiers; Abelard (1079–1142) and Peter Lombard (c.1100–1164), at Paris; John of Salisbury (c.1115–1180), at Chartres; Robert of Melun (c.1100–1166), William of Conches (c.1100–1154), Peter of Blois (1135–1204), Bernard Silvester (fl.1150), and Theobald of Canterbury (d.1161), to mention but a few.

During the twelfth century, there was much activity in monastic libraries. "A monastery without a library is like a castle without an armory." The monastic scriptorium became an active institution. The transmitters were not all transmuters, but their labors helped to preserve the tradition of Christian humanism. For the most part, the handwriting still possessed the legibility of the Carolingian minuscule; but Gothic strokes and cursive writing became more common. This century also saw a revival in the art of the illumination of manuscripts, with beautiful initial letters in red, green and gold. And there was a growing mastery of design and fine stamping of the leather bindings.

"From the fall of the Roman Empire down well into modern times," writes Haskins, "the Latin classics furnished the best barometer of the culture of each period in the Western Europe. Never wholly lost from sight, their study rose and fell in close relation to the general level of education and intellectual activity." The classical revival of the twelfth century manifested itself in a wide reading of Latin authors (especially the poets) and in commentaries on them. The highest representative of this culture was John of Salisbury (c.1115–1180), who had been trained in the best schools in the north of France. With John of Salisbury, there is no sense of antagonism between classical and Christian; the two elements are fused in a well-rounded Christian humanism. He was the most scholarly product of the school of Chartres whose tradition was maintained by the great Breton brothers, Bernard and Thierry, and the Norman, William of Conches. Orleans, perhaps, came second as a literary center (where Virgil, Ovid and Lucan were held in high esteem) but it cannot boast classical scholars like Bernard of Chartres or John of Salisbury.

In the twelfth century, men prayed and sang, taught and preached, traded and communicated in a Latin that implied a thorough drill in Latin grammar and even a scholarly appreciation of literature. The standard text-book, the *Institutiones* of Priscian of Caesarea (fl.500), was filled with citations from Roman scholars. Its eighteen books carried on the traditions of Latin litera-ture as well as of grammar.

The twelfth century made its own dictionaries and encyclopedias, for example, the *Lexicon* of Papias, the *Panormia* of the Englishman Osbern, the *Derivations* (c.1200) of Hugutio of Bologna (d.1210). All three paid much attention to etymology and to Greek roots. *Dictamina* or *Artes Dictaminis* (manuals on the art of writing) were multiplied. This classical revival was far more than a mere revival of ancient modes and sub-jects; it was a manifold expression of the vigorous and many-sided life of the age, which was one of reason and romance, revelry and a strong religious spirit. The Christian humanist could do something with Latin which neither the pagans of antiquity nor the neo-pagans of the fifteenth century ever achieved. The spiritual élan which they put into their soaring architec-ture inspired the emotional cadences of their verse. Not even Cicero could weep and laugh in Latin, as these men did. As Henry Osborn Taylor puts it:

> Christian emotion quivers differently from any movement of the spirit in classic measures. The new quiver, the new shudder, the utter terror, and the

utter love appear in mediaeval rhymed accentual
poetry. . . .

Let any one feel the emotion of these verses and
then turn to some piece of classic poetry, a passage
of Homer or Virgil, an elegiac couplet or a strophe
from Sappho or Pindar or Catullus, and he will realize
the difference, and the impossibility of setting the emotion of a mediaeval hymn in a classic metre.[3]

The best known of the poets of this century, the one
who has assimilated most fully the spirit as well as the
form of Latin poetry, is Hildebert of Lavardin (1055–
1133) [4] Bishop of Le Mans. Archbishop of Tours and
man of action, he was equally at home with the Muses.
Having ridden to Rome as a statesman and bishop, he
weeps over the ancient ruins in verses which reveal the
music of classical meter and the mood of Romantic
melancholy.

> *Par tibi, Roma nihil, cum sis prope tota ruina;*
> *Quam magni fueris integra fracta doces.*
> *Longa tuos fastus aetas destruxit, et arces*
> *Caesaris et superum templa palude jacent. . . .*
> *Hic superum formas superi mirantur et ipsi,*
> *Et cupiunt fictis vultibus esse pares.*
> *Non potuit natura deos hoc ore creare*
> *Quo miranda deum signa creavit homo.*
> *Vultus adest his numinibus, potiusque coluntur*
> *Artificum studio quam deitate sua.*

Thou hast no peer, O Rome, though prostrate in these
    ruins;

[3] *The Classical Heritage of the Middle Ages* (N. Y., 1925),
pp. 246–47.

[4] See F. J. E. Raby, *A History of Christian-Latin Poetry* (Oxford, 1927), pp. 265–273.

For fragments spell the splendor of thy past.
Age has subdued thy pride, and Caesar's palaces
  Lie with the temples of the gods in slime. . . .
But gods themselves look down upon these statues, longing
  For features half as fair as men have made.
Could nature ever make her gods with forms so fair
  As man has given to his gods in stone?
Divine such features are; but call for reverence,
  Not for their godhead, but the art of man.

These verses are rightly considered as a high-water mark in twelfth-century classicism.

Abelard, brilliant dialectician and teacher, was also a poet.[5] In a group of beautiful hymns composed for the nuns of the Paraclete, he shows a great variety of forms, from complicated meters to the simplicity of the following:

> *Est in Rama*
> *Vox audita*
> *Rachel flentis,*
> *Super natos*
> *Interfectos*
> *Eiulantis.*

> There is heard
> A voice in Rama
> Rachel weeping,
> Broken-hearted
> For her children
> Massacred.

This was the great age for secular Latin lyrics. The Goliardic poets, gay and disreputable, yet scholars of a sort, reflect their *joie de vivre* in lines like these:

[5] Raby, *op. cit.,* pp. 319–326.

Meum est propositum in taberna mori,
Ut sint vina proxima morientis ori.
Tunc cantabunt letius angelorum chori:
"Sit deus propitius huic potatori."

In the public-house to die
Is my resolution;
Let wine to my lips be nigh
At life's dissolution:
That will make the Angels cry
With glad elocution
"Grant this toper, God on high,
Grace and absolution."

Another essential part of this "Renaissance" was the
revival of Roman law and of jurisprudence. This was
closely related to the economic awakening in the Medi-
terranean world. From one university to another,
Roman law was ordinarily carried by some traveling
professor who lit the torch of learning in a new place.
Historiography also became popular. Chronicles, an-
nals and lives of the Saints abound in the twelfth century. Norman England produced a succession of remarkable biographers and historians: Eadmer (1060–
1124), Ordericus Vitalis (1075–1145), William of
Malmesbury (1095–1142), Henry of Huntingdon
(d.1154), Geoffrey of Monmouth (d.1155), William
of Newburgh (1135–1200), Roger of Hovedon
(d.1205), Geraldus Cambrensis (1147–1220) and
many others. Many scholars came under the spell of
Arabic learning: Adelard of Bath, Plato of Tivoli,
Robert of Rétines, Hermann of Carinthia, with his
pupil Rudolf of Bruges, and the most prolific of all
Gerard of Cremona; also a group of Jewish scholars,

Petrus Alphonsi, John of Seville, and Abraham ben Ezra. Toledo became the center of this new Arabic learning.

An intellectual revival occurred in the domain of science and above all in philosophy. With the trivium and quadrivium thus filled out with the new logic, new mathematics, new astronomy, law, medicine and theology, it was inevitable that a new creation in the field of educational institutions should arise—the Universities.

MEDIEVAL UNIVERSITIES

The publication of *Die Entstehung der Universitäten des Mittelalters,* in 1885, by the Dominican, Father Denifle, and that of the *Chartularium Universitatis Parisiensis* (1889–1897), by the same author in collaboration with M. Chatelain, disclosed a mass of information concerning the enormous cooperative effort of medieval scholars to organize knowledge during the twelfth, thirteenth and fourteenth centuries. This information has been extended and brought up to date by F. M. Powicke and A. B. Emden in their edition of Rashdall's *Medieval Universities.*

Europe was dotted with university centers which, cementing the continent into an intellectual league of nations, profoundly affected the progress and intellectual development of the West. This peculiarly medieval creation depended very slightly on what belonged to the pagan world. Neither the Chinese, Japanese, Arabs nor any people of the ancient world had achieved such educational organization. It was the resultant of many Christian minds of different nationalities working corporately toward a single intellectual end.

No one boasted of being an Englishman at Oxford, an Italian at Bologna, a Frenchman at Paris. There was no talk of nations except for the purpose of organizing the social side of academic life. Professors and students were citizens of Christendom, imbued with an international sense which was stimulated by frequent traveling from one university to another.

This corporate humanistic effort helped in the development of representative government and democracy. For example, in Paris, as many as 10,000 students, sons of princes and peasants, mingled in a common fraternity and shaped a social system that helped to level all classes. A man of brains could rise from the lowest class of society to the most privileged political or ecclesiastical position. A large percentage of the Popes and statesmen of the Middle Ages were men of a lowly parentage. The thirteenth century heard little talk about social equality, but saw much of it in fact.

Nevertheless, discipline was the essence of medieval education. If the educators of the thirteenth century (unlike those of the twelfth) seemed less devoted to the literature of antiquity, it was because they discovered the disciplinary value of logic and philosophy. Thomas Aquinas did not receive as complete a humanistic education as John of Salisbury, but his powerful mind was trained in the new philosophic mold of his century. It was this discipline that made possible the fifteenth-century "Renaissance," by training the minds and stimulating the very curiosity that later was to seek out and rediscover so many of the classics.

The causes of this movement are significant. The material cause (to speak in the language of the Middle Ages) was the accumulation of the ideas pooled by all the previous centuries. The formal cause (that which made it specifically what it was) came from the corporative tendency that was in the air during these centuries: the instinct to wish to belong to a corporate body—a guild, a faculty, a religious order. The efficient cause of the movement varied. From its origin, there were two classes of universities: 1. Universities *ex consuetudine,* such as Paris, Bologna, Salerno, Coimbra, with their migratory offshoots: Oxford, Cambridge, Padua. 2. Universities *ex auctoritate.* This second type of university might be a Papal foundation such as Toulouse; an imperial foundation, such as Naples; a national one, such as Palencia; or a communal one such as Florence.

The social aspect of university life in the thirteenth century presents a gay picture. This is represented in the boisterous Goliardic verse of the times, which reveals the scholar wandering from school to school, "light of purse and light of heart," joyous and carefree. To answer the needs of this social life, numbers of local colleges sprang up in large cities. These colleges, although units in themselves, belonged to the great world of university life and were often endowed residences provided for poor students by generous founders.

Scholasticism

As the medieval universities produced an outer pattern of European educational method or, rather, were themselves the product of the medieval urge to produce such a pattern, so there was, in the Middle Ages, an impulse to produce an inner pattern of ordered thought that might serve as a map in the mind for all Western men.

Scholasticism is the name of this impulse. It is, essentially, the idea that the most native hunger of the human mind is for an ordered synthesis of knowledge, whether that knowledge arises from sense experience (science) or reflection (philosophy) of Divine Revelation (theology). The fundamental faith of the system is that an integration of all these forms of knowledge is both possible and, intellectually, imperative. The integration, as it was finally conceived by St. Thomas Aquinas in the thirteenth century, is the culminating achievement of medieval culture.

From the point of view of method, Scholasticism is the application of rational principles of human thought to Revealed Truth in an effort to widen the frontiers of knowledge by perceiving, as far as is possible to human intelligence, the inner meaning of supernatural Mysteries; and, at the same time, to elaborate a synthetic, organic system of all those truths that have relation to human life, both here and hereafter. The technical pedagogical method was that of the *disputatio*. Each thesis that claimed admittance to the system was made to serve as a battleground for the clash of many minds; it was allowed to enter only through the door of debate between doctor and doctor or students and masters.

Unlike a good deal of modern discussion, these medieval debates accepted three definite points of reference, three recognized courts of appeal. The first was the authority of Revelation, the right of Divine Wisdom to a hearing from the human mind. The second was the right of Reason, especially of the principles, processes and products of corporate reasoning, to guide individual speculation. The third was the argument from Tradition, the idea that where corporate thinking has proceeded over many generations, it is likely to have eliminated a good deal of error. *Securus judicat orbis terrarum:* the mind of the whole world does not easily err.

This appeal to authority was, of course, open to abuse. A certain amount of "theologism," dialecticism and obscurantism was as fatal then as "scientism" and "progressivism" can be fatal today. It becomes easily possible to exaggerate one or another tendency inherent in a system so rich. In the twelfth century, a school of dialecticians represented by Berengarius of Tours tended to over-rationalize Faith; while in the fourteenth century both nominalism and mysticism tended to underrate the role of reason.

But in its best representatives, Christian philosophy achieved a fruitful marriage of Faith and science as unlike anything in antiquity as Christian architecture, Christian painting, and Christian poetry, in Notre Dame de Paris, in the St. Francis of Giotto, in the *Divina Commedia,* are different from the parallel products of pagan genius. Prayer and worship proved to be faithful ministers of intelligence, conscience and taste, so that whatever was true or good or beautiful lifted the soul to the Truth and Goodness and Beauty of God.

In the *Paradiso* of Dante there is a symbolic representation of the diversity of tendency in the Scholastic system. In one great circle in Heaven of the Sun, Dante sees the "rational" spirits: Thomas Aquinas (1225–1274), Albertus Magnus (1193–1280), Gratian (fl.1140), Peter Lombard (1100–1164), Dionysius the Areopagite (fl.500), Orosius (fl.415), Boethius (475–525), Isidore of Seville (c.560–636), Bede (674–735), Richard of St. Victor (d.1173), and Siger of Brabant (fl.1270). Beyond these, in a second circle, he sees the "seraphic" spirits: Bonaventure (1221–1274), Illuminato and Agostino (followers of St. Francis), Hugh of St. Victor (d.1141), Petrus Comestor (d.1178), Petrus Hispanus (Pope John XXI, d.1277), Nathan the Prophet (fl.950 B.C.), Chrysostom (347–407), Anselm (1033–1109), Donatus (fl.330), Rabanus (c.776–856), and the Abbot Joachim of Floris (d.1202). Still beyond these he seems to discern dimly a third circle of those who, presumably, like himself sought to synthesize still more perfectly seraphic light and cherubic love.

Concretely, of course, Scholasticism is a part of that general historical phenomenon we call the Middle Ages. It is the sum of the several systems of philosophical and theological speculations which were developed throughout the Christian centuries, and particularly by the *scholastici* (or school teachers) of the twelfth and thirteenth centuries.

It may be traced ultimately to Patristic thinking in the first four Christian centuries. In St. Augustine (354–430), it had a real "founder." Without his synthesis of Faith and reason, his linking of Platonic thought with Christian revelation, the history of medieval thought would have been very different. In the centuries after St. Augustine's, the two intellects that contributed most were those of Boethius in the sixth and John Scotus Erigena in the ninth. In the eleventh and twelfth centuries, St. Anselm and Abelard led the vanguard of thought. With the beginning of the thirteenth century came the fuller knowledge of Aristotle's works, through the translations from the Arabic writings in Spain. It was a short step to St. Thomas Aquinas. With him, medieval Scholastic philosophy reached the zenith of its splendor. After him, it began to decline.

St. Thomas Aquinas

St. Thomas appeared in a century that was favorable to his architectonic type of genius. Centralization was a main historical force of the age. New sources of thought had been opened up by translations of Greek and Arabian philosophers. A new organization of studies had been systematized at the Universities. New religious Orders and especially the Mendicants had been recently founded, and a group of eminent contemporaries were illuminating the age: Alexander of Hales (d.1245), Albertus Magnus (1193–1280), Bonaventure (1221–1274), Raymund of Pennafort (d.1275), Roger Bacon (d.1294), Vincent of Beauvais (d.1264), and others.

The century of St. Thomas was an era of controversy. The gradual transition from the humanism of

the twelfth century to a sharper intellectualism had
brought in its train the need to synthesize conflicting
tendencies. Two schools had taken definite shape. The
Augustinians, or Platonists, stressed the primacy of the
will. They believed that the important thing in life is
what is loved, and that the mind has immediate knowledge without the aid of the senses. The Aristotelians
emphasized the primacy of the intelligence. They believed that the important thing in life is what is thought,
and that the soul, as the form of the body, depends upon
the senses for its knowledge. St. Bonaventure and
the Franciscans belonged to the first school; St.
Thomas Aquinas and the Dominicans to the second.
Dante has bestowed praise upon them both, in his
eulogy of their founders:

L'un fu tutto serafico in ardore,
L'altro per sapienza in terra fue
Di cherubica luce uno splendore (Par., xi, 37–9).

The one was all seraphic in his fire;
The other by his wisdom on the earth
Showed forth the splendid light of Cherub choir.

At the age of three, Thomas was sent to a Benedictine monastery where he remained until he was twelve.
There he was taught grammar and the classics and was
imbued with a wise placidity. Frederick II insisted the
youth be sent to the University of Naples, which had
been founded in 1224, as a rival institution to the Universities of Bologna and Paris. Here Thomas came
under the influence of Peter the Irishman, whose subtle if undisciplined mind stimulated his illustrious pupil

with a real love for Aristotle. Later Thomas, now a Dominican Friar, was sent to the University of Paris to continue his studies, and here attracted the attention of one of the greatest masters of Europe, Albertus Magnus. From Paris, both Albert and Thomas went to the University of Cologne, where the former lectured and the latter became his most illustrious disciple.

Aquinas was now ready for lecturing. As a *baccalaureus biblicus,* he taught the Bible for two years; as *baccalaureus sententiarius,* for two years more, he lectured on the *Liber Sententiarum* of Peter Lombard and wrote his own *Commentarium in Librum Sententiarum.* Then as a *magister docens,* he remained at Paris, until summoned by Pope Urban IV to the University of the Roman Curia.

Of his more than sixty volumes, the *Summa Theologica,* composed between the years 1267 and 1273, is the greatest. It is a monumental work, with thousands of details concatenated to form a complete and harmonious pattern. The ordering of the *Summa* seems as natural as the unity of a tree with its roots, trunk, branches, leaves and blossoms growing together. It is divided into three parts. The *Prima* (first part) is a consideration of God as Being and as the Origin of Being, as Life; the *Secunda* treats of God as the End and Purpose of man, as Truth; the *Tertia,* of God as the Means of bringing men back to Himself, as the Way.

In the *Prima,* four sections discuss the Unity of God, the Trinity, God as Creator, and God as End. The first question is that of the existence of God *(an sit).* The question of the essence of God *(quomodo sit)* is followed by a study of His Attributes: Simplicity, Perfection, Infinity and Immensity. Next comes a luminous explanation of God's Knowledge, Love and Power—the three Divine Operations which are constantly in the foreground throughout the *Summa*. In the second section, the three Divine Persons are considered separately: the Father, as Principle, Being, Cause, Agent; the Son, as the Word, Image, and Wisdom; the Holy Ghost, as Love. There follows an attempted explanation of the relationship between the three Persons. When God thinks, the Thought is not, as with us, a passing accident; it endures as a permanent subsistent Person. God thinks the whole of knowledge, not just a single notion but Infinite Truth; hence, the Divine Thought is God Himself, the Second Person of the Blessed Trinity. The Divine thinker and the Divine Thought fall in love with each other, not as we love, fleetingly, but by an act that *is,* that subsists as the Person of the Holy Ghost, eternally, as a permanent Love. When God the Father thus thinks and wills, there is no further act of the Godhead to achieve another permanent Person. Thus there are three and only three persons in the Blessed Trinity.

In the third section, there is a consideration of Creation and the production of creatures. An analysis of created beings follows: souls alone—as angels—composed of intellect and will, whose entire activity is thinking and loving; bodies alone—as matter—endowed with mere passivity; bodies and souls—as men —composed of intellect, will and matter. Man is a unity; the soul is the "form" of the body, not a mere lodger, exile or prisoner. In the fourth section, there is an explanation of the direct action of God and of the indirect action, by means of angels, bodies and men.

The *Secunda* is divided into two parts. In its entirety, it is a treatise on the acts and means whereby man, a creature endowed with free will, directs himself towards God, his End. The *Prima Secundae* discusses the End of man—his Eternal Beatitude; the means to this End of ultimate Truth and Goodness; human acts and the passions of love, hate, desire, joy, pain, sadness, hope, despair, fear, courage and anger. Besides the intrinsic principles of human acts, which are good habits (virtues) and evil habits (sins), the extrinsic principles are explained—law, in its three forms, eternal, natural, human. The *Prima Secundae* concludes with a treatise on Grace considering it in its nature, essence, divisions and effects.

The *Secunda Secundae* deals with the moral obligation of man. The three subdivisions correspond to the three important means of reaching God: the theological virtues, the cardinal virtues, states of life. In the first of these sections, there is an analysis of the virtues of Faith, Hope and Charity, and of the opposed vices and of the corresponding gifts of the Holy Spirit. In the second section, the same plan is followed as regards the virtues of prudence, justice, fortitude and temperance. In the third section, St. Thomas gives an analysis of the active and contemplative lives.

The *Tertia* treats of God as the Way and comprises three treatises: on Jesus Christ in the Mystery of the

Incarnation and in the Mysteries of Life; on the Sacraments, in which Christ communicates His Grace to man; on the four last things. As St. Thomas died before he completed the work, a supplement taken from his earlier writings is printed in all modern editions of the *Summa Theologica.*

THE DIVINE COMEDY

The *Summa Theologica* is far too difficult a book for the average reader. It is not, therefore, ever likely to become a practical introduction to an understanding of medieval culture. It is different with the *Divine Comedy.* Although no modern translation has yet been able to communicate more than a fraction of the meaning and music of this medieval masterpiece, it can still be enjoyed in several English renderings.

Dante's life and works constitute the best possible approach to an understanding of medieval humanism. His life is the best answer to those who still imagine that the world had to wait till the fifteenth century for what Burckhardt described as the full blossoming of the individual, *die Entwicklung des Individuums.* Dante's age is likewise the answer to the other illusion of Burckhardt that the Discovery of Man and the World, *die Entdeckung des Menschens und der Welt,* was made at the time of the discovery of America.

It would be difficult to imagine a fuller life than that of Dante Alighieri. Born in 1265, already in 1274 (the year of the death of St. Thomas Aquinas and also of St. Bonaventure) he was deeply in love. By the time he was eighteen he had taken his place among the poets of his day. To love and literature he added learning. He mastered Latin not merely in a way that enabled him to write a fluent Latin prose, but so thoroughly that in his declining years he could turn from writing the *Divine Comedy* to the composition of Latin *eclogues* in Virgilian hexameters. For three years he studied philosophy under both Dominican and Franciscan teachers, and began a course of philosophical reading that achieved an extraordinary mastery of Aristotelian and Thomistic thought. Meanwhile he took a part in all the fun of the young folk of Florence. Every canto of the *Paradiso* is a witness to the fact that Dante must have given a great deal of time to dancing, singing and music. One of his sonnets could only have been written by a man in love with hunting. His constant use of metaphors taken from archery tells us of a life in the open air. He fought as a soldier. For seven years he took an increasingly important part in the politics of that most fiercely competitive of all medieval democracies; and he rose at last to be one of the *priori* or supreme governors of the city of Florence. He served as ambassador to the Pope. When he fell from power, he was not merely exiled, but was threatened with death should he dare to return. In his exile, he traveled not merely in Italy but almost certainly to France and possibly to England and Germany. There is some evidence that he studied at the University of Paris in the years from 1307 to 1309. His letters to Cardinals and even to the Emperor reveal him not merely as a Florentine or an Italian but as a genuine citizen of Christendom.

And as a part of his life we must reckon his creative

literary activity. His *Vita Nuova,* which tells of his love for Beatrice, is one of the most delicate and original of autobiographies, at one and the same time, realistic, romantic, religious. His *Convivio* is a banquet of philosophic, historical and literary essays of a kind that had never been attempted in any other European vernacular. In the *De Vulgari Eloquentia* he turned to philology, and wrote in Latin. The *Monarchia* is a closely reasoned discussion in the field of political philosophy. In a somewhat quaint work called *De aqua et terra,* he not merely showed himself at home in all the technique of medieval discussion, but revealed a genuinely scientific curiosity. And, finally, there is the *Divine Comedy.*

But the sources of Dante's happiness were far deeper than external activity. What makes him a humanist was his passionate pursuit of goodness and beauty and truth, his quest for happiness through love and art and wisdom.

Dante was a lover of a unique kind. It was as a lover that he defines the quality of his art:

> I am a man who, when
> Love whispers to the heart, takes note and then
> Retells the tidings to the rest of men.

> *I' mi son uno che, quando*
> *Amor mi spira, noto, e a quel modo*
> *ch' e' ditta dentro vo significando* (Purg., xxiv, 52–54).

These tidings Dante has conveyed to us, for the most part, under the name and symbolism of Beatrice. There is, first of all, in the literal and historical sense of the opening chapters of the *Vita Nuova,* his romantic love

for little Bice Portinari, the dear girl who first made
the tiniest pulses of his heart tremble, as he says, "hor-
ribly": the Beatrice who at sweet seventeen, with a simple bow, could transport young Dante's soul to the very
"limits of beatitude." There is, secondly, an ideal Beatrice, the "young, young angel," the *angiola giovanis-
sima,* who seemed to Dante, in one of the few Homeric
phrases that he quotes, "not a mortal but the daughter
of the gods." And it was because of this ideal, I take it,
that we may believe him when he says that his romantic
passion was absolutely pure, at all times tempered (as
he puts it) by the faithful counsel of his conscience. It
was this double Beatrice whom he saw in the strange
vision which went to the making of the first verses
which he ever cared to keep.

> At first, the Lord of Love seemed gladsome, keeping
>   My heart within his hand, and on his arm
> My lady covered with a cloak and sleeping.
>
> Then, wakened, of my heart with flames upleaping
>   She ate, in lowliness and much alarm.
> Then, Love I watched go on his way, a-weeping
>   (*Vita Nuova,* iii).

There is, thirdly, a Beatrice in the mystic, anagogic
sense, the Beatrice that kindled in the soul of Dante
the love of God. This is the Beatrice of the last lovely
sonnet of the *Vita Nuova,* the Beatrice, already in
Heaven, visited by a sigh that issued from Dante's sor-
rowing heart, the Beatrice too divinely dazzling to be
seen and yet too like the real and the ideal not to be
recognized, not to be discovered, at least in dumbness,

by desire. I have never been able to get the right rimes
to make an English sonnet of that song; but some faint
echo of the rhythm and meaning may be gathered from
the following lines:

> Beyond our space and all the spheres in motion
> Passes the sighing of my sorrowing heart;
> Over the waters of which skiey ocean
> Love, and love only, plies the pilot's art.
>
> Then when it reaches where desires surrender,
> Seeing the Lady of this starry goal,
> Her radiance of light and heavenly splendor
> Capture the senses of my pilgrim soul.
>
> Not but the mind were baffled to recover
> Sights past the power of memory to hold
> Did not my dumbness, in desire, discover
> A tongue to utter what the Vision told.
>
> This (for so much the mind remembers) this
> Lady of the Dream was Beatrice
>
> (*Vita Nuova,* xli, 10).

It was when Dante had sung that song that he saw
the Vision that was to inspire the *Commedia.* He saw
such things, he tells us, as made him wish to sing no
more of this Blessed Beloved until he should be more
fit to sing her praises. And so he writes in a prose that,
in the Italian, has all but the music of poetry:

> And to come to that I study all I can, as she right
> truly knows; so that, should it be His will for whom
> all things live, to give me a few more years on earth,
> I hope to sing a song such as never was sung of

another. After which may it please Him who is the
Lord of Love to let my soul go forth to see the
glory of this Lady, my blessed Beatrice, who now,
in Beatific Vision, looks into the Face of Him who
is Blessed for ages without end (*Vita Nuova,* xliii).

As all the world knows, God gave to Dante those
few more years on earth; and the Song was sung. Dante
called it a Comedy: the world has called it Divine. In
it the poet passes from beauty to beauty, and truth to
truth, and goodness to goodness, until at last the eyes
of his spirit gaze at the Beauty and Truth and Goodness of God. But what we can never forget is that the
Divine Comedy is a love poem about Beatrice; it was
she who taught Dante to lift himself from love to love
until he could love that Beauty beyond which there is
nothing for the heart to long for,

> *Ond'ella a me: "Per entro i mie' disiri,*
> *che ti menavano ad amar lo bene*
> *di là dal qual non è a che s'aspiri . . . . .*
> (Purg., xxxi, 22–24).

One thing, I think, is clear. So far as fullness of love
is a part of a humanist's life, Dante would seem to have
a very real claim to the title.

To speak, as I have just done, of a Dante passing
from beauty to beauty, and truth to truth, and goodness
to goodness until the eyes of his spirit gazed on the
Beauty and Truth and Goodness of God is to imply
that Dante the lover was, likewise, an artist, a philosopher, a moralist and mystic. And to say this is to link
him with what has been characteristic in each of the

great modern movements in the history of the human spirit; with the Renaissance revival of classical taste and our contemporary cultivation of conscience, to both of which the word humanism has been conventionally applied; but also with the Reformation regard for Grace and the *Philosophe* attention to intelligence and the Romanticist claim for the place of passion in human life. And to say this is to emphasize once more the integral or synthetic character of medieval humanism in contrast with a humanism that was too exclusively esthetic in the Renaissance or too exclusively religious in the Reformation, or too rationalistic in the age of Voltaire, or too sentimental in the early nineteenth century, and today is too exclusively ethical.

Humanism, in other words, has in the modern world become, like Religion, sectarian; we have one humanism for the artists, another for the Saints, a third for the thinkers, another for those who feel, and finally one for the followers of what Mr. Santayana has called the "Genteel Tradition." It was otherwise with Dante. He was a humanist who managed to embrace all our modern enthusiasms.

He shares with the Renaissance its love of beauty; he was an esthetic humanist. More simply he was an artist. He was an artist in so universal a sense that he has never seemed more modern than he does today. And yet there is about his whole theory of art something specifically medieval.

First of all, he is a creationist. He is convinced that beauty whether in the things of Nature or in the thoughts of Man is nothing if not a reflection of Beauty as it is in God. Everyone recalls his pregnant line, *vostr'arte a Dio quasi è nepote* (Inf., xi, 105). That is to say that human art is, as it were, a grandchild unto God. What he means is that artistic vision is born of objective beauty which in turn is born of God; all archetypal Beauty, the Idea as Plato would say, is in God. By creation, the Idea becomes realized as "form." This "form," shining forth from the "matter" in union with which all non-angelic forms exist on earth, is what the artist sees. Beauty, to Dante as to St. Thomas, is the *splendor veri;* as any one may read in the moving words of St. Thomas himself in the thirteenth canto of the *Paradiso.*

In the second place, Dante the artist is definitely Scholastic in his metaphysical acceptance of the hierarchy of being and in his psychological recognition of the degrees of abstraction. In some sense it may be said that, artistically, the *Inferno,* the *Purgatorio* and the *Paradiso* represent Dante as, respectively, a mere poet, a metaphysical poet, and a mystical poet. In the *Inferno,* passionate vision is mainly aware of scenes and sounds as reported by the senses and imagination; in the *Purgatorio,* the poet is moved more by thoughts, by reality perceived in abstraction stripped of the outer clothes of matter and individuality; in the *Paradiso,* the vision is, if anything, more passionate than ever, and therefore more poetic, but so penetrating that it reaches beyond the world of matter and sensation, beyond the world of the human mind and its normal thoughts, to the world of the Mysteries revealed by God. What is apparent in all three *cantiche* is the sustained and passionate perception of beauty in a medium of music that never fails the poet even when he is singing of the Ultimate Beauty in terms of the utmost abstraction. He complains, of course, as all mystical poets must, that words are too short to reach his thought, and thought too weak to hold his vision; but the test of artistic vision is the joy it gives, and this remains with Dante to the end.

There are many illustrations in the *Commedia* of Dante's insistence on the hierarchy of being (and therefore of beauty) and on the degrees of abstraction (and, therefore, of poetical penetration). Thus every reader of the *Paradiso* has surely remarked that vision deepens and joy is heightened as the elements of sense diminish. In the first planet, Piccarda appears with every detail of sensible appearance as though she were seen in a mirror; in the next planet, Justinian is perceived as a shadow in a field of light, as a kind of silhouette; in the third planet, Carlo Martello is nothing but an undimensional light; still higher the veil of beauty grows ever more tenuous until there is nothing but "an intellectual light all shot with love"; and finally the unveiled beauty of God is seen face to face.

So, too, in the *Purgatorio,* on the first terrace it is carvings in marble that speak to Dante's mind, very marvelously indeed and beyond the power of nature and earthly art, as Dante said, since the carvings were not only seen but heard. Sculpture played the part of drama; it was "visible speech," *visibile parlare.* On the second terrace, without sensation the message comes directly to the mind; it is an invisible voice that utters "courteous invitations to the feast of love." On the third terrace there is a more mysterious message that comes neither from things nor from thoughts. What Dante hears is heard in ecstasy, a message immediately from God without the medium either of matter or of the abstracting mind.

Besides creationism and Scholasticism in Dante's art there is another element common to all medieval art. It is sometimes called allegorism; but its proper name should be, I think, "anagogicism." It was not enough for Dante that a poetic myth written for the imagination should imply a message for the mind, that there should be both a literal and an allegorical sense in the songs he sang. There is room in supreme art, he thought, for four senses, the literal, the allegorical, the moral and the anagogic. Besides the myth and the meaning there should be a lesson for the will and a lift for the spirit, a moral and an intimation of supernatural Mystery, an intimation of what Dante calls "the supernal things of Eternal Glory" (*Conv.*, II, i, 6). Thus in the *Commedia* the myth of Beatrice is an allegory of Revelation and a lesson to bad ministers of Revelation, in particular to bad Popes; and, finally, an intimation of the Mystery of the Incarnation. One of the loveliest scenes in the whole *Commedia* is the descent of Beatrice into the Chariot of the Church in the thirtieth canto of the *Purgatorio*. In the anagogic sense it is a lightly veiled account of the coming of Christ, in the Incarnation.

Some of these aspects of Dante's art have seemed to certain modern critics to be out of date. Nevertheless, taken all together, these aspects reveal a Dante seeking for beauty in three worlds and in three ways and for several reasons; and if that multiple quest brought him human happiness, as it surely seems to have done, then it gives to Dante another claim to rank among the humanists.

The same may be said, I think, for Dante's quest of happiness through truth; that is to say, for Dante as a philosopher, and even (though this is more debatable) for Dante's quest for happiness through holiness; that is to say, for Dante as a Saint. At any rate Dante did not greatly distinguish the artist, the philosopher and the Saint. The first is passionately in love with beauty; the second passionately in love with truth; and the third passionately in love with goodness. All of them, radically, are in love with God as the sole ultimate source of all beauty, all truth, all goodness; with God, that is, as the Author of all Order, whether esthetic, or metaphysical, or ethical.

Belief in Order, you may say, is Dante's fundamental Credo. He saw everywhere with his senses the order of parts to wholes: the designs, the plans, the proportions, the harmonies that make the face of the world so fair. He saw deeper with his thought the order of natures and ends, the purposes and final causes: the teleology that gives the world its meaning for the mind. And with his Faith, quite fully, and partly with his reason, he saw more than outer plan, more than immediate purpose; he saw the ultimate Providence of God lifting the rational meaning of human life to the mysterious level of a Divine destination.

All this Dante puts into the mouth of Beatrice as she

and Dante begin the ascent from the planets through the stars to the Empyrean and so to God.

> All things [she says] without exception are part of one vast whole, and Order is the form that makes the universe like God. In this Order all things have their place, according to their nature and their end, some nearer to and others farther from the Source from which they spring. And so it is that all things move across the one wide sea of Being, but yet to different ports, each thing sailing by its own specific purpose (*Par.*, i, 103–114).

Not, of course, that in this world of plan, purpose, Providence, that is to say of law (or as Dante and the Middle Ages preferred to say of love), there is no place for liberty. Order is not merely physical and metaphysical but also ethical. There is an order not only of means but also of merits; and therefore the will is free. This is what Beatrice has in mind when she says:

> And yet, just as in art the form achieved does not always reach the ideal that was dreamed, because the material is deaf to the artist's call; so from the path proposed by Providence, those creatures that have the power of choice depart at times and swerve at will to other goals, if they are drawn by seeming good; much as, in the case of lightning, fire whose tendency is to go up may be seen hurrying to earth (*Ibid.*, 127–135).

Thus the Cosmos, as Dante sees it, is not, as it were, a circle with a single center, but rather an ellipse with a double focus. The shape of life is determined not only by law but also by liberty. It is thus that Dante the philosopher reaches towards his definition of man. Man is not merely an animal; man is a rational animal, a being in whom the light of reason can reconcile the liberty of his will with law of his lower nature.

But man, as Dante sees him, is not merely a rational animal; he is a social animal. He is not only the master of his soul; he is a member of society. He has an exigency for fellowship; he needs the home in childhood, the school in adolescence, the State in manhood. This State, however, is neither the Leviathan of modern Materialism nor the illusion of modern Idealism. The State, as Dante thought of it, is so subordinate to Man that civil liberty and civil law must be based on moral liberty and moral law, that is to say, they must be related to the human personality.

If Dante as a pure philosopher understood that the person must be free, as a political philosopher and a philosopher of history he understood that the person must be under law. The end is the person; the necessary means of his perfection are liberty and law. Both are needed for man's peace and man's perfection, that is to say for man's highest human happiness; and both are linked, therefore, with what seems to me the fundamental character of a genuine humanism. Looked at historically it may be said that Dante's insistence on the need of law links him with what is essential in the classicism or classical humanism of the seventeenth century; while his insistence on liberty links him with whatever was soundly human in the spirit of the French Revolution.

Nevertheless man, in Dante's conception, needs

something more than liberty in his soul and for his soul, and something more than law in social living. The fact is that man is more even than a rational and a social animal; he is an image of God destined for a supernatural end, for the utter fullness of his mind in the Vision of God and the correlative love and fruition of a soul in immediate union with the Goodness and Beauty of God.

But if man is destined for such Glory in a life to come he has need of Grace in his life on earth. It is this insistence on the need of Grace that makes of Dante a religious humanist; but not in an exclusive sense. Man needs both law and Grace, both reason and Revelation, both prince and priest, or as Dante would say, both Emperor and Pope. Only so can man hope for both temporal and eternal peace.

It is this conception of man as both a rational animal and an image of God that gives meaning to that epic of man and that program of integral humanism which he called the *Commedia*. In that song, God is Alpha and Omega, the beginning and the end, the cause and the consummation both of the soul of man and of the society of the Saints. Under the form of a myth about a man journeying through Hell, Purgatory and Heaven, Dante offers us the sublimest of all allegories of the double mystery of human liberty and Divine Law, of man's free choice and God's inscrutable Justice.

But it is no Greek tragedy of human nature defeated by a Divine necessity. It is a Christian comedy of human freedom wooed and won by Divine favor. Dante in the poem expresses man in all his needs and in the fullness of his human nature. The Dark Wood is a picture of human passion. The rescue by Virgil is a symbol of the role of reason and the rule of law. Virgil's voice is the wisdom of an ideal and universal Empire. The descent of Beatrice is a symbol of the role of Revelation and the help of Grace. She is the supernatural wisdom of a divinely guided, Catholic Church. Two other guides that fill a great part of the *Purgatorio* represent, so at least it seems to me, the role of learning in the School and of love in the Home. Stazio is the Christian teacher and Matelda is the Christian mother. There remain two other guides. Cato is to Virgil somewhat as Bernard is to Beatrice. Cato is law not in the State but in the soul, that is to say he is conscience; he is that which makes us spiritually free as Virgil is that which guarantees our social freedom. Bernard is Grace, not as given through the channels of the Church, through Revelation and the Sacraments, but as given immediately, mystically, to the soul; he is supernatural intuition.

It is this Epic of Man that gives to Dante his clearest claim to the title of integral humanist. It is a humanism that by starting with the obvious assumption that God is the Creator of both Man and Nature reconciles all those elements that modern disintegration has torn asunder.

We have spent the modern centuries in reckless wars, making enemies of art and religion, passion and reason, liberty and law; as though a man could not love at the same time both beauty and Grace, order and ardor, the new and the old. We may learn from Dante that if we are to be fully happy in a human way we must cultivate intelligence, conscience and taste, in the light of both reason and Revelation, and with the force of both passion and Grace; and all that, because man is, as Dante said, the horizon between Nature and God. Dante, therefore, should not be called either the herald of the Renaissance or the father of the Reformation, or a Classicist or a Romanticist, or the heir of Holy Roman Imperialism or a prophet of the French Revolution. Nor is he any combination of the spirits of these movements, as an artist-saint or a passionate Puritan. His proper title is a medieval or Christian humanist.

BIBLIOGRAPHICAL NOTE

THERE is no completely satisfactory account in English of the nature and historical development of medieval humanism. In order to acquire some sense of the vitality and variety of medieval cultural life one has to master the elements, one by one, of medieval scholarship, philosophy, poetry, architecture, political theory, law, science, vernacular literature and so forth.

A good introduction is Sir John Edwin Sandys' *History of Classical Scholarship* (Cambridge, 1903–1908), Vol. I. This will help the student to grasp the continuity in the use and adaptation of Latin (and in part Greek) thought and language, in spite of the so-called decline and fall of the Roman Empire. Sandys' work should be supplemented with J. Westfall Thompson's *The Medieval Library* (Chicago, 1939). (For certain reserves in regard to this work, see my review in *Thought,* XV, March, 1940, pp. 146–148.) Medieval poetry can be studied in two works of F. J. E. Raby: *A History of Christian Latin Poetry from the Beginnings to the Close of the Middle Ages* (Oxford, 1927) and *A History of Secular Latin Poetry in the Middle Ages* (Oxford, 1934); although it has to be borne in mind that, in reference to the Middle Ages, the distinction between "Christian" and "secular" is often highly misleading, since in many cases the same men wrote both "Christian" and "secular" poetry, and since there was practically no "secular" poetry in the modern, negative, sectarian, agnostic or atheistic sense.

It is well to pass from the study of poetry to that of philosophy and theology, in order to note how frequently the "poets" are likewise "philosophers" and "theologians." This comprehensive universalism and resistance to mere departmentalization is so characteristic of medieval humanism that some effort must be made to understand it. A safe introduction to the study of medieval philosophy is M. de Wulf's *History of Mediaeval Philosophy* (London, 1925–26), supplemented by Etienne Gilson's lectures on *Christian Philosophy* or, at least, by Gilson's *Reason and Revelation in the Middle Ages* (New York, 1939) or *Christianity and Philosophy* (New York, 1939). For those who can read German, it is well to reinforce the conception of the magnitude of the medieval philosophic effort by such a work as *Die Patristische und Scholastische Philosophie,* by Dr. Bernhard Geyer (Berlin, 1928). The extensive bibliography in this work is particularly valuable.

Even the non-specialist should read some works on law and political philosophy. The monumental work of R. W. and A. J. Carlyle, *A History of Mediaeval Political Theory* (6 vols., Edinburgh and London, 1903–1936) will dispel any idea that political thought was in any way static or uniform in the Middle Ages. Again, such a work is important in revealing how literary humanists or even poets, like John of Salisbury or Dante Alighieri, could be passionately preoccupied with the problem of the State. A most important essay by O. Gierke, *Political Theories of the Middle Ages* (Cambridge, 1900), must be mentioned. Used with caution, W. A. Dunning's *History of Political Theories, Ancient and Mediaeval* (New York, 1902), is still serviceable; as is also *The Social and Political Ideas of some great Mediaeval Thinkers,* edited by F. J. C. Hearnshaw (New York, 1923). For the latter part of the Middle Ages, there is the work of Father Bede Jarrett, O. P., *Social Theories of the Middle Ages 1200–1500* (London, 1936). The work of Professor P. Vinogradoff (edited by the Catholic scholar F. de Zulueta), *Roman Law in Medieval Europe* (Oxford, 1929), brings out still further evidence of the continuity of the ancient and medieval worlds.

Some study of Christian architecture (like the study of Christian philosophy and Christian poetry) is needed to emphasize the specifically Christian "soul" of medieval Christendom. In this connection, no other work quite equals E. Mâle's *Religious Art in France* (New York, 1913), supplemented by Mâle's other volumes which have not yet been translated, *L'Art religieux de la fin du Moyen Age en France* (Paris, 1908) and *L'Art religieux du XIIe Siècle en France: Etude sur les Origines de l'Iconographie du Moyen Age* (Paris, 1922).

A good deal of scholarly research is now being devoted to medieval science. Here again what is important to notice is that the "scientists" were often enough philosophers, theologians, bishops or even Saints. A good introduction is Haskins' *Studies in the History of Mediaeval Science* (Cambridge, 1924).

Most directly concerned with humanism is the study of medieval education, and in particular of the medieval universities. *Rashdall's Medieval Universities,* edited by F. M. Powicke and A. B. Emden (3 vols., Oxford, 1936), is indispensable. But this should be supplemented by the work of the Catholic scholar, Stephen d'Irsay, *Histoire des Universités,* Tome I, *Moyen Age et Renaissance* (Paris, 1936).

Works on particular periods throw much light on the general nature of medieval humanism. P. de Labriolle's *History and Literature of Christianity from Tertullian to Boethius* (New York, 1925) should be read in order to note how vitality was given to Latin letters in Christian circles at the very time when Latin paganism was doing nothing of note for creative literature. An excellent study of an important transition period is Miss Eleanor Duckett's *Latin Writers of the Fifth Century* (New York, 1930). Of capital importance is E. K. Rand's *Founders of the*

Middle Ages (Cambridge, 1928). For those who read French an indispensable work is G. Kurth's *Les Origines de la Civilisation moderne* (Brussels, 1923). This should be compared with Christopher Dawson's *The Making of Europe* (New York, 1932). For the period 500 to 900, M. L. W. Laistner's *Thought and Letters in Western Europe* (New York, 1931) is excellent. On the twelfth century "Renaissance" the classical work is now C. H. Haskins *The Renaissance of the Twelfth Century* (Cambridge, Mass., 1927).

The two most notable efforts to present, in English, a synthetic study of medieval culture are Henry Osborne Taylor's *The Mediaeval Mind* (London, 1911 and many subsequent eds.) and the translation from the German of Karl Vossler's celebrated introduction to the study of Dante, under the title, *Mediaeval Culture* (2 vols., New York, 1930). Vossler's work should be used with caution. (See my review in *Thought*, V, Sept., 1930, pp. 328–334.) Taylor's work is still the best general introduction to the study of the development of thought and emotion in the Middle Ages. He gives a great many more illustrations than could be even alluded to in this short sketch of the Hellenic, Roman, Teuton, Celtic and specifically Christian elements in medieval humanism. Yet it is doubtful if Mr. Taylor ever quite felt, in personal experience, what is meant by the "soul" of Christendom. This is the more singular, since he speaks with confidence of the "soul of Hellas" and of the "soul of Latium." He understands even that "the soul of Latium" could "imbue" many diverse lands with "a new homogeneity of civic order" (p. 4) ; yet he never quite admits that the Catholic creed and code and culture could be other than something that "had been superimposed upon paganism" (p. 8). It is as though he could see the soul of Christendom only through the kaleidoscope of the modern mind. Remembering this, one can better understand the shortcomings of an otherwise admirable book.

ABSTRACT FOR STUDY AND REVIEW

I

The Tradition of Christian Humanism

THE root idea of humanism is that every one has the right, if not the duty, to seek human happiness in a human way. And because Christ, in His human nature, "grew in wisdom and age and grace with God and man," Christian humanists in all ages, without neglecting the supernatural life of Grace, have felt free to pursue, with taste and intelligence the Greek ideal of beauty and truth and, in the light of conscience, the Roman ideal of justice and goodness.

II

The Roots of Christendom

Medievàl humanists sought a synthesis of Hellenic light, Roman law and Christian love with German force and Celtic fancy.

The first problem was for the Christian intelligence to reconcile wisdom and Grace, reason and Revelation, philosophy and Faith. St. Augustine (354–430) is a supreme example of a Christian Hellenist.

The second problem was for the Christian conscience to reconcile whatever was good in Roman civilization with the Christian code of morals. A Christian Roman like St. Ambrose (340–397) could pass without difficulty from the work of a Roman Governor to that of a Christian Bishop, and could transform a pagan book like Cicero's *De officiis* into a treatise on Christian ethics.

So it was that the Christianized Roman Empire never really "fell." In spite of much material destruction and even cultural decline, the roots of an enrichment of life were sown when the emotionally and imaginatively vigorous peoples of the North were brought within the frontiers of Christendom.

III

Light in the Dark Ages

After the dark winter of each period of barbarian irruption there was a bright second spring, a revirescence of culture. When Charlemagne gave political peace to Europe, Christian humanists abounded in Europe. Before and after the age of Charlemagne, the British Isles maintained almost unbroken a tradition of humanism attested by the works of Bede (d.735) and an epic poem like *Beowulf*.

IV

Medieval Humanism

Both in Britain and on the Continent, even in the darkest hours, a succession of schoolteachers kept alive a tradition of scholarship, sanctity and song. Even in far-off Saxony a nun like Hrotswitha has left us Latin verse and drama full of striking passages of force and fancy.

The eleventh century saw the beginning, and the twelfth century the full blossoming, of a cultural revirescence. Remarkable teachers like Fulbert of Chartres and philosophers like St. Anselm prepared the way for integral

Christian humanists like Hildebert of Lavardin and John of Salisbury. The Latin poetry of the age, combining classical meter and taste with medieval music and emotion, reveals to us rich personalities drinking from deep wells of happiness.

The climax of medieval humanism is reached in Dante Alighieri (1265–1321). His stupendous and original creation, the *Divine Comedy,* could only have been conceived and written by one who was able to encompass all aspects of life and love and learning. Dante, in fact, was not only a poet but a soldier, a politician, a traveler, a philosopher, a theologian and, in some sense, a mystic. His life was made possible by the development of Scholasticism in the universities, of poetry in Provence and Sicily, of piety in the religious Orders and of political life and thought in communes like Florence, in nations like France, and in the Holy Roman Empire in Germany and Italy. His life teaches us that "to be fully happy in a human way we must cultivate intelligence, conscience and taste, in the light of both reason and Revelation and with the force of both passion and Grace."